# FACTORY FOR GOOD

# Factory for Good

*The Pitfalls of Prosperity and How to Avoid Them*

**ALEX BEAN**

ISBN 979-8-9908036-0-2 (hardcover)
ISBN 979-8-9908036-1-9 (ebook)

Printed in China

Printed by Book Printers of Utah

*factoryforgood.com*

**fac·to·ry for good**
/ˈfakt(ə)rē/ fər ɡood/

1. the entity through which you input your time, energy, and resources to produce a positive, lasting impact.
2. a tool that uses Purpose, Relationships, and Legacy to create a sustainable impact and get on the path to true happiness.

**pit·falls of pros·per·i·ty**
/ˈpit͵fôls/ /əv/ /präˈsperədē/

1. hidden or unexpected difficulties associated with being successful in material terms

# CONTENTS

**REFERENCES**

**ACKNOWLEDGEMENTS**

# Foreword

I've studied and taught about influence and "crucial conversations" for 35 years. There are few things that influence a family for good or ill more than money. And there is nothing more dicey to discuss than money.

This book is an invitation to both unflinching consideration of the influence you want money to have in your life, and to forthright conversation to support your aspirations. Alex Bean is both morally and intellectually qualified to write it because he is engaged in the same ongoing self-examination and is doing so as thoughtfully as anyone I know.

*Factory for Good* is more than a manual on avoiding the pitfalls of prosperity. It is that, to be sure. But it is also both a mirror and a map, reflecting common struggles and illuminating a credible path to genuine fulfillment. In my work, I've observed that the most transformative dialogues are those that challenge us to redefine what we mean by success. Alex does this vulnerably and persuasively. He offers a crucible that distills vast life experiences into the essence of what truly matters: purpose, relationships, and legacy.

You'll groan with recognition as Alex takes us through the unexpected trials of unanticipated wealth. You'll pause to reflect as he frames prosperity as stewardship as much as privilege. And I think you'll love to experience his humor, respect, and empathy.

Reading this book gave me tools not just for managing money but for enriching lives through deliberate and meaningful action. It's a testament to the power of intention in crafting a life that goes beyond the accumulation of wealth to generate lasting happiness and impact. I recommend this book to anyone who has been fortunate enough to taste success and is wise enough to anticipate its influence. If you already know in your bones that money doesn't guarantee happiness, what follows will help you be deliberate in becoming its master rather than its slave.

**JOSEPH GRENNY**

*CO-AUTHOR OF CRUCIAL CONVERSATIONS*

*CO-FOUNDER AND CHAIRMAN OF THE OTHER SIDE ACADEMY + THE*

*OTHER SIDE VILLAGE*

*UNITUS LABS*

# Prologue

Think about the first time you produced value from your own creations. Was it a lemonade stand on the side of the road? Making friendship bracelets? Delivering newspapers? Or maybe babysitting? The pride of earning your own way in life is as real as it is exhilarating. I discovered this for myself when I was growing up, from teaching swim and ski lessons in high school to failed businesses in my college years (more than I'd care to admit), and still more businesses after college—some that failed and some that had success. An entrepreneurial spirit has always been a big part of my identity and has been a guiding force in many of the decisions I have made in my life.

We each have it in us to build and create value, first as a measurement of survival and then as a measurement of success. Because of this shared instinct, I can safely assume that at some point in each of our lives, we aspired for more—to have resources to build and create, to better provide for our family, to help us actualize a great dream, or even to make the happiness we are all looking for. In many cases, this aspiration and dedication are admirable and even needed to progress through this life. However, if we're not careful, we can start tying our worth to how much we have and how much money we can make, putting ourselves firmly in a never-ending race.

Money is an amplifier of both good and bad.

Money changes things, and more money changes more things. It's not just your life that changes—it's the lives of everyone in your circle, from yourself to your partner, your kids, your friends, and potentially for generations to come. While money is often celebrated as a source of happiness, it's not one. It's a currency, and it's up to you to choose what you want to do with it.

I've seen it do amazing things in the hands of amazing people and families, but I've also seen it ruin many amazing people and families. It has a way of revealing and even amplifying someone's character. I want to be one of those people doing amazing things with money. I don't want to have spent my whole life working for something so hard just for it to end up ruining my family.

When used irresponsibly, you quickly realize how dangerous money can be. Like alcohol, it suppresses your conscience, so your subconscious—who you are at your core—becomes louder. Money is very much a drug as it permits us to let go of inhibitions. It can be very powerful but also very poisonous. While many resources are available to handle the logistical side of things, such as wealth advisors, banks, and industry experts, few resources help with the emotional side of finances. And the tools to help manage these emotions are less accessible. What many don't realize is that there is a wide array of pitfalls associated with prosperity that can be difficult to navigate.

This became real to me when, together with an incredible team, we built and sold a tech company called Divvy. When we sold the company, I was surprised by the many emotional difficulties that came with the money. I found myself asking:

*Why am I less happy now that it's over?*

*Why do I miss the stress of working?*

*Why do I feel such a loss of identity?*

*Why is my marriage suddenly more complicated than it was before?*

*How can we raise our children to be responsible and not entitled?*

I was struggling here, and I had no one to talk to about it. It was incredibly lonely. I knew where I wanted to end up but had no idea of how to get there. I looked around for guidance and direction and found no clear source to help me navigate my emotions.

But I did see countless examples of people doing great things with their money and others who seemed to be completely ruined by it. Their contrasting experiences, coupled with my own, prompted this book.

In it, I explore how to navigate the pitfalls of prosperity and design your life to become a Factory for Good—a tool to create lasting and sustainable impact and get on the path to true happiness.

I set out to read, study, and interview as many people as possible who are doing it right and some who are doing it wrong. I was interested in discovering why some people do great things with the money they have earned while others appear to be ruined by it. While I've changed their names for privacy, this book is built on the stories of those who have "done it." I leveraged my experience and my family's, read dozens of books and scientific studies, and interviewed hundreds of builders, business owners, and founders. I don't know all the answers, but this research helped me identify examples of what works and what doesn't work when trying to build a lasting impact, or as we call it, a Factory for Good.

As I chose which stories to include, I purposefully drew from the extremes—using stories of individuals who have experienced stark excess in their lives. This helps paint the picture of money as an amplifying force, and the extremes show us what happens when we leave the emotional side of money unattended. It is through the extremes that the lessons become apparent and applicable to whatever stage of life we are in. Likely, each of your lives isn't as extreme, but the principles and lessons can still be applied. Most importantly, the extremes warn of the dangers that come if you do nothing.

The factory analogy and the retooling process I explore can be applied at any stage of life. Still, when your basic needs are met, and you have excess at your disposal, these frameworks and the consequences of not living them also become amplified.

For those aspiring to reach the summit of success, those who are at the peak, and even those who reached the peak years ago, it's never too early or too late to start to shape your life into a production of good, impacting both yourself and those around you. Scientific studies consistently show that individuals often feel more fulfilled and whole in their lives when they engage in activities that help others or produce positive outcomes. This sense of fulfillment comes from a variety of psychological and physiological benefits associated with altruistic behavior. Helping others can significantly enhance one's sense of purpose and meaning in life.

For example, a study by Roy Baumeister found that while happiness is linked to receiving, meaning in life is more strongly associated with giving and helping others. For instance, offering support to others in emotional distress can enhance the helper's own emotional regulation and reduce symptoms of depression. This reciprocal benefit is seen in various settings, from casual acts of kindness to more structured volunteer work.

Given these findings, whether you are a high-net-worth individual or someone in a middle-income bracket, focusing on creating a "Factory for Good"—an initiative or project dedicated to generating positive impact—can be a key component of a fulfilling life. This approach not only benefits the recipients of your good deeds but also enriches your own life through enhanced meaning, better health, and stronger social connections.

My message is especially applicable to those fortunate enough to have resources available. As you'll see, the stories of those who don't navigate the pitfalls purposefully are consistent and many. This is a plea to not succumb to the classic pitfalls of consumerism. In doing so, I hope to help you move through the emotional side of money and find "true" success.

Above all, my message is intended to provide what I didn't find when I first transitioned from Divvy: a safe space to have this conversation and really dig into its difficulties. This process has taught me profound lessons about my family's history and the legacy I want to create. Recognizing the positive examples in the stories I highlight in the book, I'm inspired to follow in their footsteps, ensuring that my wife and I raise our children with the same values of intention, love, and connection. This project has not only transformed my outlook on life but also has filled me with excitement for the possibilities ahead.

I hope I have provided frameworks to help you navigate the pitfalls of prosperity and clearly outline how to build a Factory for Good. As you consciously look at your purpose, relationships, and legacy and use the presented frameworks to maximize your impact, you will be able to find yourself, as I have, on a path to deeper fulfillment.

# | 1 |

# The Factory

This is the story of two men. The first grew up in a small rural community, the eldest of five siblings. The family had little at the time, so he tried to contribute wherever he could—raising lambs and rabbits and selling them for pennies. With few resources available, he often had to be creative and find his own entertainment, like when he built a wagon and joyfully coasted downhill, sharing the exhilarating experience with his friends.

When he was eleven, his father's unexpected death catapulted him into the role of primary breadwinner. With no jobs readily available and several small children at home, his mother could not work, leaving him alone in his mandate to provide for his family— which he did for the rest of his life. The wagon he once built to ride down hills with his friends was now the tool he used to support his family, as it was used to carry firewood. These small endeavors taught him formative lessons in independence and self-sufficiency, and he discovered great satisfaction in both.

At age twenty-one, he sacrificed a college education. Instead, he left home and worked in a neighboring city so that he could afford to send his four siblings to college. He prioritized others' well-being, working tirelessly to support their education. He found work as an accountant for the Skaggs company, a small firm that eventually birthed retail giants such as Safeway, Payless Drugstores, Osco Drug, and American Stores. Seeing greater opportunity in sales than in accounting, he took a significant pay cut to build up "Skaggs Store #42" in Salt Lake City. He and his team worked tirelessly, often starting at 5 am and returning home at midnight.

Soon, his hustle paid off. Within months, he was managing his own store. In a few years, he was overseeing stores in four states. Stories of him during this time are countless: he beat the competition by bringing fresh citrus to town, was robbed at gunpoint, and outsmarted an exploitative coal company by opening his store at night so miners could shop under the cover of darkness. Despite the worst years of the Great Depression, he managed to keep his stores open and thriving.

He was no stranger to heartache, however. By the late 1930s, his health had deteriorated from working so hard, and the company he had devoted himself to replaced him. Jobless, he lost everything he had earned and had to climb back up from the bottom.

After searching for a few years, he found an opportunity in a small drugstore. Through massive effort, his business expanded across the entire Western U.S., outperforming the competition with its new chain of spotless stores filled with merchandise at fair prices. Within a few decades, more than 300 stores were scattered nationwide.

He was a highly skilled businessman who achieved great success. His dedication to business filled him with deep purpose. However, it wasn't the foundation of his stores that filled him with the most pride but the formation of a family that loved him dearly. Later in life, he still looked out for his siblings, giving them jobs and involving them in his business endeavors. He deeply loved his wife and children, prioritizing quality time with them. When he could afford nice things, he shared them, letting family and community members spend time at his vacation home and with his fishing boat. He found further fulfillment in the outdoors, eventually channeling this passion into funding a natural history museum that has prolonged his legacy of good. Now visited by thousands each year on a university campus, the museum features rich stories and encourages visitors to connect with the earth's environment. His life's work, balanced across the pillars of purpose, relationships, and legacy, culminated in lasting happiness.

The second man had a different upbringing. Born before the Depression, he was brought up in a home where he wanted for little, but despite being well-off, he wasn't entitled. His parents did well in cultivating thrift and hard-working habits in him.

He was the class president kind of guy, an athlete, and naturally charming—traits that made him popular in school. He had the gift of interpersonal skills, and wherever he went, he was well-liked. He carried these characteristics into military service, where he served with distinction in some of the worst battles in the Pacific Theater of WWII. During the war, he demonstrated that he was always a leader and a businessman—he was quickly promoted to sergeant and he built up his savings by sending money home from cigarette stipends that he didn't use each month and by purchasing a camera to charge other soldiers to take their pictures with their local girlfriends.

Shortly after returning home, he contracted polio—a crippling disease that altered his trajectory in life. No longer able to rely on his physical strength, he was determined to sharpen and improve his acumen, which he applied to his business endeavors to get more from the resources available. He worked extremely hard, creating where needed and doing so with flair and optimism. He built a team to assist, taking his business aspirations to new heights. He was extremely involved, and he became the natural leader in every organization he became a part of. He even helped establish an organization dedicated to the eradication of polio.

However, his business quickly became his primary focus. Even at family events, he would intently read news about his business endeavors. He was distant from his four children, rarely participating in their activities or supporting them in school and extracurricular events. His constant distraction put a strain on his marriage, which ended in divorce.

Perhaps his desire to "build and grow" overpowered his judgment, for in time, he exposed his business to takeover hawks who ultimately swooped in. All he had driven for and found purpose in was gone. Furthermore, a life dedicated to empire-building left him with personal, worldly wealth but with limited family relationships. His children scattered, many falling victim to the pitfalls and vices that money often enables. His second wife and two new children remained distant from his older children and friends. After twenty years of marriage, he ended up broken and alone.

When his health began to decay due to old age, his second wife, not wanting to care for him, placed him in a nursing home. She only visited him twice a month for hour-long visits out of obligation. On his deathbed, she changed his will so that she would inherit everything, leaving the rest of his family, charities, and a beloved lifelong secretary with nothing. Three of his four children were caught in their own trials and never got around to visiting him in his final years. After abandoning his greatest cheerleaders and supporters, his life ended alone in a nursing home.

The two men from these stories are intimately connected.

They are father and son.

And I know them as my Great-Grandpa ML and Grandpa Monte.

Their experiences were at the front of my mind when I walked similar paths in my life and career. I worked from job to job, learning where I could and always looking to improve. I had a clear purpose: to provide for my family. It was a challenge, but I enjoyed it and felt pride in my daily effort. Through trial and error, many failures, some luck, and much work, I experienced success when, together with an incredible team, we built and sold a tech company.

When I exited, my life reached a natural fork in the road as I considered meaningfully: who do I want to be? More specifically, how can I live a life like my great-grandpa and avoid the outcome of my grandpa? How do I structure my life to make sure that I make a positive impact in the world instead of succumbing to the pitfalls of prosperity?

In wrestling with these questions, I concluded that each life is like a factory.

A factory has inputs and a clear output. In life, we input our time and effort to produce the essential product for the factory to run smoothly. Like a factory needs raw materials, maintenance, and energy to run, our life factory needs safety, shelter, and food to survive.

Every day, as soon as you wake up, you go to your "factory," where you spend your time and energy. You work hard, caught in the daily operations of your life factory. You are responsible for your factory's output, which depends on the choices you make in how you spend your energy and time. Initially, money is your critical output, motivated by the need to fulfill necessities. It is what sustains you and your family's needs.

So, day in and day out, you work extremely hard to input time and energy and watch as money, the resource that fills your needs, is produced.

When you move from survival mode to when your basic needs are consistently met, a decision arises—where do you spend the excess? This moment is a trigger point for deciding what's next for your factory. For the first time in your life, you have the option to retool your factory and make a choice as to what your factory will produce.

If left undecided, your money-producing factory will continue to produce money. There is no ceiling to how much you can make. But there is danger in allowing production to continue without guidance. Ultimately, it leads to a lousy output, as exemplified by my grandpa and countless others. Continuing to produce only money without a deeper purpose can lead you to stagnation or unfulfillment. Yes, money is powerful, as it can buy you attention, influence, distraction, and fun, but if money is the only output in your life, you will be left with nothing.

The good news is that you have a choice. By consciously retooling your factory, you can ensure that it ends well.

You can transform your life's factory from a money-making machine into a source of good, leveraging your accumulated resources to enrich your life and the lives of others in more profound ways. To retool a factory, you consciously take your output—money—and convert it into an input to use as your amplifying force for good. As you carefully run your time and effort, amplified by your money, through purpose, relationships, and legacy processes, you can successfully produce Good. The more Good you create, the more successful you are, or the happier you will be. This is in direct contrast to when money remains the measurement of success, and happiness is an elusive commodity. In short, you can build a Factory for Good and tap into a source of lasting happiness.

## Monte vs ML

I have examples of both choices in my own recent family history. Grandpa Monte built a factory that produced exactly what he set out to create—money. He didn't realize that money was better served as an amplifier to make a Factory for Good. Though he had many admirable characteristics and drove forward with diligence and intention, he lost his bearings. His focus was on acquisition and growth, which he achieved, and that is something to be celebrated. However, he did so at the cost of his family life. His problem with money was presuming that it was the happiness he sought. He missed the mark, never realizing all the good he could've done with it if he had moved to be his input or a source to help him with a true output. Instead, it remained his focus and ultimately led to his demise.

He was someone who, on the surface, had everything you could ever want, and though he reached all of his goals, he tragically died alone with nothing left. His factory's output—his lasting impact—was shallow. What I find most tragic is that his story was so close to being like a fairytale. He was the epitome of accomplishing the American dream. He excelled at building and creating. He worked hard, took appropriate risks, and built an empire. Unfortunately, his story did not end in "happily ever after." It ended in sadness.

I want to avoid ending up like him, so I know I can't follow a similar path.

On the other hand, I want to be like my great-grandfather, ML. Although I haven't met him, I honor him—my entire family does. He lived purposefully, enjoyed many loving relationships, and left a legacy of service to family and community that resonates to this day. He could have done those things without money, but he made a lot of it and made superb use of it. For him, money was an amplifier of everything good. He successfully amplified his factory inputs, and his output was simple—it was Good. This collective good brought him lasting happiness and a positive and enduring impact.

## Navigate to Where You Want to Be

After building our company, I realized money could be a blessing for me and my loved ones, and I sincerely hoped it would increase my happiness. Still, there was also a significant risk that it could lead to my family's destruction. I recognized my enormous responsibility in managing the emotional side of money because many people's lives would be affected by where I placed my focus and my values now that I could retool my factory. Based on the contrasting experiences of my great-grandfather and grandfather, I was painfully aware that if I didn't make the right choices, consumerism, carelessness, or just plain entropy might devour what matters in my life. I was in desperate need of some guidance.

Sea navigators will tell you you'll lose your way unless you keep your eye on three key landmarks: a lighthouse, a mountain, or a star in the distance. If you "triangulate" your position to those three landmarks, you can always tell where you are. Likewise, when navigating the design of your life into a Factory for Good, you should always maintain sight of purpose, relationships, and legacy.

This book is the blueprint for how to create a Factory for Good. These are the three landmarks; if you follow them, as you input the same amount of time and effort, amplified by your money, you'll produce lasting happiness. If you carefully keep purpose, relationships, and legacy in balance, you will arrive where you want to be.

Through these actionable pillars, I hope to help you create your own blueprint: a framework that will help you serve a purpose that is meaningful to you, maintain high-quality relationships, and leave a legacy of opportunity for generations to come. Ultimately, in doing so, you will successfully avoid the pitfalls of prosperity and navigate closer toward fulfillment and happiness—the direct result of creating your Factory for Good.

# PURPOSE

"Happiness is not in the mere possession of money; it
lies in the joy of achievement, in the thrill of creative effort."

**- FRANKLIN D. ROOSEVELT**

# | 2 |

# Earning Your Sleep

The happiest people on earth know their purpose and fulfill it. The definition of this purpose has captivated philosophical and theological discussions for decades. Great philosophers and ordinary people alike have pondered what truly makes us happy and what our purpose in life as humans should be.

Aristotle believed that every person has a 'telos' or an ultimate purpose. In his work *Metaphysics*, he suggests that the act of creation is part of fulfilling this telos. When we create, we actualize our potential, and in doing so, we find our purpose. According to this belief, it is in our human nature to build and to create.

Examples of creation fulfilling purpose and creating joy are all around us, from small children engaging in play to impoverished communities innovating to improve their lives. These examples teach us that happiness is not tied inextricably to money but can be found in creating and building. With something to actively build or create, it's easier to find direction in life.

This principle became tangible to me a few years ago during a particularly stressful point in building our company, Divvy. We built Divvy from the ground up, and it was challenging. My partner and I were constantly testing and iterating. It felt like we were playing a continuous game of whack-a-mole. Every time we solved one problem, another would always spring up.

Three years into building, we had grown to 400 employees, and our growth was skyrocketing. Out of nowhere, COVID-19 hit, and like the rest of the world, everything came to a grinding halt. Financing fell through, which created immense uncertainty. We were scared that we were going to go out of business. We had to strip the company down to its core to survive, letting go of some really talented people in the process. This made it necessary to learn to do more with fewer people and still scale quickly. There was a real chance we would lose it all. It was painful, scary, and easily one of the most stressful times of my life.

Gradually, things started to look up. Some things started going our way, and we continued to work hard. I began to see a path to potential buyers. I was optimistic, but there were no guarantees. The tiny hope I had became my compass, and I was entirely focused on that point on the horizon where I could leave it all behind.

During this time, I took a rare break and went golfing with friends. I found myself with a couple of guys, one of whom was named Jake. Having inherited lots of resources, Jake never needed to work for a living. Reliant on his inheritance, he had all the time in the world to do whatever he wanted.

Jake didn't waste his days partying, which I deeply respected. On the surface, he led quite an idyllic life. He had a loving wife and family and was involved in several projects to improve his self-mastery and enjoyment in life. I envied his freedom, having the time and resources to do anything he wanted, which seemed like a dream come true. At that time, just having a moment to breathe seemed amazing. I fantasized about getting through the exit and enjoying that kind of freedom.

As we talked, I described all the stresses I was experiencing and conveyed the excitement of moving towards a thrilling goal. While I described the opportunity to challenge myself, Jake expressed that he was envious of my daily effort.

Gradually, I realized something fascinating: while I couldn't wait to be him, there Jake was, living the apparent dream, and yet he wanted to be me. He had everything that I was working towards, and he still felt like his life was lacking something that I was taking for granted. I wondered in amazement,

*How could that be possible?*

I realized that despite having the "freedom" I longed for, Jake still wasn't happy. He didn't have something to keep his mind occupied while in traffic, think about in the shower, or keep him up at night; nothing producing wins and losses that he could share with his family at the end of the day. Jake had spent much of his adult life searching for this happiness, but he didn't have something in his life that made him feel like he had "earned his sleep."

That day, I gained some valuable perspective. It hit home for me that my dream of working so that I could do nothing someday was hollow. I realized the power of purpose is the power of having something meaningful to build. It is the fantastic feeling of "earning your sleep" at the end of the day. Without that kind of fulfillment, there is no lasting happiness.

However, when I exited my business and could do nothing, I quickly learned this was easier said than done. I had every intention of living a meaningful life. To fill my days, I made a list of items to do and eagerly crossed each off my list. Some of the things were really fun and I had dreamed of doing them for a while. I lived for the high of each thing completed. However, the sensation became dull and less exciting as I crossed more items off. I found myself wondering why it wasn't fulfilling anymore.

One night, I tossed and turned, unable to sleep. While questioning why this was the case, I remembered my interaction with Jake and discovered I couldn't sleep because I wasn't progressing. I was just doing "stuff." I realized what was missing: I needed to build and create. That sleepless night helped me realize how hollow my life had become. While pursuing each item on my list was often enjoyable, I felt a sense of emptiness at the completion and was left wondering:

*What can I do to find happiness?*

While wrestling with this inner conflict of lack of purpose, I was invited to participate in events for a local charity. Over time, a relationship developed. I involved my kids in the charity and eventually donated exercise equipment for the students. As I got feedback from the charity, showing the students using and enjoying my equipment, I started to feel some fulfillment.

I was amazed to find that this—looking outward—brought me an even higher high than the best items on my list, and it was an incredible feeling. It wasn't the shallow or fleeting feeling I had experienced when buying goods or experiences. But when I felt the joy of giving, loving, and sharing, that "high" was unlike anything I had ever experienced.

This inspired me to find my cause, something I am deeply passionate about. I began establishing a factory that would produce a clear purpose for life, a vehicle to cultivate my closest relationships and leave a lasting impact on my community. It's a work in progress, but I already feel the difference in my life. As I use money as an amplifier and intentionally apply it to a higher purpose, deeper relationships, and a lasting legacy, I hope to be left with a single output: Good.

If you've left a business to enjoy its fruits or find yourself in a time of a general financial transition, you may feel, as I did, that you are no longer needed in the same way as before. You may have lost your core identity as a leader, problem-solver, or decision-maker. With this identity loss, you likely have lost focus on a clear purpose to drive your day-to-day life. It's possible, even probable, to un-knowingly and inadvertently fall back on acquiring money to drive your actions. If you ultimately end up on this path, like my grandpa, you will alienate family and friends and find yourself alone.

Luckily, we always have power over our purpose. The exciting part is that we get to choose what we will create. When money comes and life shifts, we can find purpose based on our truest and deepest priorities. The key is to use money as an amplifier to fulfill a meaningful purpose rather than to replace it as the central focus.

Let me illustrate what I mean.

In 2011, Hadley Impact executively produced the *End of Polio* campaign. Using the convenor method of philanthropy, they brought together several different NGOs, including Rotary International and the Global Poverty Project, to focus their collective attention on a single effort: eradicating polio. They conducted a giant campaign in which they invested over $1.5 million to fund event producers and celebrity ambassador acquisitions, support a live audience of over 4,000 people at a signature event, and establish online marketing channels.

Money made all of this possible, and the culmination of all these efforts resulted in increased government funding, matched by private donations from the Gates Foundation, to equal an amount of $118 million for their cause. They secured 118 million donated vaccines. All of this was only possible with the initial $1.5 million overhead. By investing this money and focusing its attention and efforts, they multiplied the amount of money donated and the impact for their cause many times over. Money was a clear amplifier of their effects on a higher purpose and cause.

However, you don't need millions of dollars to leverage to make an impact. For example, Scott Harrison, though not considered wealthy by many standards, leveraged his resources in a way that made an even more significant impact.

Scott began his career as a nightclub promoter in New York City, living a life far removed from philanthropy. However, a trip to West Africa, where he volunteered as a photojournalist for a humanitarian organization, changed his perspective entirely. Witnessing the dire need for clean drinking water and the suffering it caused, Scott was moved to dedicate his life to solving this crisis. He established charity: water, a nonprofit organization dedicated to providing clean and safe drinking water to people in developing countries.

By providing access to clean, safe drinking water, Scott significantly impacted the lives of millions of people. Although he didn't have any of his own money to spend, Harrison revolutionized fundraising in the nonprofit sector by pioneering innovative donor engagement and transparency approaches. Charity: water's unique funding model ensures that 100% of public donations go directly to funding water projects, while private donors cover operational expenses. Through the establishment of charity: water, Scott found a deep purpose and showed that you don't need millions of dollars at your disposal to do good in the world.

When you actively focus your attention on a higher purpose—a guiding factor beyond the mere acquisition of money—your money can become an amplifier for Good. This is why purpose is one of the three central pillars of establishing your Factory for Good. It's a crucial component to finding lasting happiness.

When I felt a loss of purpose, I didn't have a path forward to help me navigate my way back toward a meaningful life. It took time and effort, but my personal experience, along with the interviews I conducted, revealed examples of what works and what doesn't in finding a purpose on which to focus your energy. The following chapters comprise a framework that includes some strategies for avoiding the distractions that money may enable; leveraging the resources at your disposal to help you live a purposeful life; and helping you on the path to finding something that allows you to again feel like you're "earning your sleep."

# | 3 |

# The Path to the Peak

A few years back, some buddies and I decided to hike Mt. Rainier, one of the tallest mountains in the continental U.S.. Having grown up in Seattle, I had always admired it as the tallest peak around, and a friend suggested it would be a great thing for us to try and accomplish together. The allure of the challenge excited me, and I was thrilled to join a group of old friends in this endeavor.

The first day of our hike was pretty standard. I had hiked several other trails in my life, and though the path was difficult, it wasn't impossible. I was enjoying the time with my friends and the beauty of the iconic Washington landscape before me. We paused at base camp, resting before what would be the most challenging part of our climb—the path to the peak.

We started just after midnight. I was already tired and sore but still had some inkling of energy and anticipation to get started. Everything was dark, but as we roped in, I could see our goal in the far distance—the peak of Mt. Rainier, its shadow visible against the light of the moon. We climbed for what felt like hours, and I was discouraged each time I looked up to see the peak still seemingly so far away. At one point, I saw some tiny, shimmering lights in the distance, and I asked my friend, "Are those stars?" His response was deflating. "No, those are people with headlamps closer to the peak." Exhausted, I wondered, *How can we still be so far away?*

As we continued our climb, inching ever closer to our goal, it took everything in me to move one foot in front of the other. I was entirely beat and wondered what led me to consider such a challenge in the first place. But still, I continued, spurred on by the energy of my friends who were finding a bit more fulfillment in our current situation than I was.

We arrived at our destination right at sunrise on a perfect morning. I felt a massive wave of amazement, relief, and satisfaction. The beautiful views of Washington laid out before us, wrapped in the warmth of the early morning light. I paused to take it all in. Then, I collapsed into the snow just off the trail. (Yes, this was a dramatic move on my part, but it's true). We had conquered the goal we set out to accomplish, and though I was physically depleted, I was totally content.

I had reached the summit.

My experience is not unique. We've all faced mountains, whether physical or metaphorical, and we've all relished in the victory of conquering a difficult peak. Each of us has experienced the allure of a challenge, the thrill of accomplishment, and the profound satisfaction that follows.

Sir Edmund Hillary, 60 years after becoming the first man confirmed to summit Mount Everest alongside his sherpa, Tenzing Norgay, described his motivation for undertaking the challenge of climbing:

*I mainly climb mountains because I get a great deal of enjoyment out of it... I think that all mountaineers get a great deal of satisfaction from overcoming some challenge they think is very difficult for them. [When climbing a mountain] you're so affected by the restrictions of the altitude that you never really can be completely confident that you're going to be able to overcome the technical difficulties ahead of you...[so when you finally reach the summit] your first thought [is] one of a little bit of surprise—of course, you are very, very pleased to be there, naturally—but my first thought was one of surprise.*

Imagine you are on top of the proverbial mountain...Money Mountain. There is great nobility in what you've done up to this point. The journey to financial security is steep and consuming. All your work has paid off. Like me, you are probably exhausted and pleased to have reached a summit. And like Sir Edmund Hillary, you are possibly in a state of "surprise." After resting and celebrating this accomplishment, it's time to choose your next peak.

The great management guru, Peter Drucker says of people who have done well, "They end up in one of three groups." One group retires, "but they usually don't live very long." Another group keeps trying to do what they've been doing but gradually declines; the third group is "looking for ways to contribute. They feel they've been given a lot, and they're looking for a chance to give back. They're unsatisfied with writing checks; they want to be involved and help others more positively."

These choices apply to anyone on the metaphorical peak of a life transition. As you summit your mountain, ask yourself:

*Will I continue climbing in a second pursuit?*

*Will I "retire" (or stop climbing)?*

*Or will I find a new mountain to climb?*

Exploring what lies beyond and determining your next climb can be daunting and exhilarating. The challenge is in discovering what you find meaningful. So what happens when the summit is behind you? When the quiet celebration of your accomplishments gives way to the echoing question: What's next?

For many, the instinct is to climb the mountain again! This is natural. We know the path well; it has brought us rewards. However, once you've tasted success, the same climb might not offer the same reward.

Initially, climbing the mountain is about securing basic needs: food, shelter, and safety for ourselves and our loved ones. But what happens when these needs are met, and the peak no longer presents a new challenge? Once you've reached the peak, attempting to conquer the mountain a second time may be less satisfying. The first climb was about providing sustained food and shelter for yourself and your family. Beyond this biological need, you've realized you've also achieved an important goal, something you have looked forward to for a long time. Once you've reached a level of prosperity to meet your basic needs, you may discover that continuing to climb in a second attempt feels flat.

My Grandpa Monte serves as a prime example. There were several different "ascents" —places where, having reached the peak of meeting basic needs for himself and his family multiple times, he could've stopped and decided to climb a different mountain. But, motivated by greed, or perhaps apathy, the pursuit of money had lost its nobility, and he was intent on constantly climbing again and again—always striving for that inaccessible number.

"All right," you may think, "I won't keep climbing Money Mountain; that's easy enough. But what else is there?" Just next to Money Mountain lies Hobby Hill. Here, the landscape is less about financial conquest and more about personal enjoyment and leisure. It seems an ideal respite after an arduous climb, and it's the most convenient and tempting place to be after Money Mountain. And, it's where I found myself shortly after my transition.

I found myself on Hobby Hill as I replaced my professional ambitions with personal interests like golf, piano lessons, and travel. While these activities provided temporary enjoyment and a way to fill time, they lacked the depth and fulfillment of overcoming significant challenges. I soon realized that, while engaging, these hobbies did not satisfy my need for a deeper purpose. I was disappointed but continued to meander around Hobby Hill without anything else to occupy my time.

I was amazed to discover how busy Hobby Hill was. I wasn't alone in my wandering—others were alongside me, chasing entertainment through various hobbies. None appeared deeply focused or happy; the climb was quickly getting old for many.

With no summit in sight, boredom, anxiety, and hollow living creep in, making Hobby Hill a great place to visit but not a place you want to live long-term. While hobbies aren't necessarily bad in themselves, meandering around Hobby Hill for extended periods lacks deep meaning. Some people decide to play forever, but that didn't work for me. Deep down, I don't think that works for anyone.

I realized that while Hobby Hill offers a break from the relentless pursuit of money, it lacks the deep sense of purpose and accomplishment from overcoming truly challenging peaks. The hobbies, although enjoyable, do not provide the same fulfillment, revealing that constant leisure can lead to a sense of aimlessness and dissatisfaction.

This realization compelled me to leave Hobby Hill for a more meaningful pursuit. Ultimately, I founded a new business that challenges me and provides significant satisfaction and joy. It's not about the financial gain anymore; it's about the impact I can make, the people I work with, and the purpose that drives me daily. The important thing is that I enjoy it and find it meaningful. I've again found a compelling purpose.

As we summit our personal Money Mountains, the question arises: What next? We can recognize and avoid staying on Money Mountain and meandering around Hobby Hill as we prioritize what matters most. But there is another path to avoid, an enticing but debilitating "disease of more," that derails the path to the peak.

# | 4 |

# The Disease of More

N ow you're at the summit. You've decided that you won't climb Money Mountain again, and you know to avoid meandering around Hobby Hill for an extended period. You look around, basking in the beauty of the peak, only to realize that someone is ahead of you and the others surrounding you on what looks like higher mountains. You begin to wonder, what if I haven't actually reached the summit? What if there is a higher peak? Something "more" to work towards and achieve?

Let's return to my Mt. Rainier story. As I lay in the snow, relishing our journey's completion, my brother-in-law approached me. Brimming with what I thought was too much energy at this point, he explained that although it *seemed* we had reached the peak, there was a possibility the actual highest point on the mountain was a ways further, and we needed to traverse a large area before climbing the final 50 feet or so to get there. I laughed; I thought he was kidding. He wasn't. I regretfully got out of my pillow of snow and started following him before collapsing again. I took a power nap as our entire group passed me.

Eventually, I rallied and followed my friends to what could have been the "real" peak. The walk was long and flat; there wasn't much fulfillment in what I was doing. When we reached the peak, I looked around, realizing the views at the previous peak were just as good; there was no indicator that the second peak was the "real" peak, and now we had traversed a fair distance that we would have to track back on our descent. This pursuit for more didn't add much to my climbing experience, and it left me tired and a bit hollow— it just didn't seem necessary.

This can be likened to our climb of Money Mountain. If we stay at the summit, continuing to walk and seek the "actual" peak after we have already reached a summit, we can fall into the traps of what the famous NBA coach Pat Riley coins as "the disease of more"; the syndrome of never being satisfied with what one has. In exploring the relationships between team members and their collective chemistry, Riley explains that initially, the team dynamic is positive because everyone is on the same team, playing their role and working hard without ego, with a common goal in sight: a championship.

However, the perspective shifts dramatically once they win and achieve that goal. Players quickly move from celebration and satisfaction to looking to the horizon for more. Riley explains:

"They want another championship; the players want more playing time, salaries, endorsements, and accolades. There is no peak: another level must be reached."

There is so much money and opportunity in athletics that it becomes hard for the players to reach a level of contentment. What was once a strong team connected by a shared vision and purpose has now become individual competitors striving for personal bests.

They keep looking forward, "eternally stricken by the disease of more." Tragically, it is only when the title is won, when that tremendous unifying goal is achieved, that egos and pride emerge, and the "disease of more" brings everything down.

Riley believes the "disease of more" prevented his championship NBA team from reaching the playoffs the year after their first championship win. "What was once a cohesive group of hardworking men begins to fray. Egos get involved. Gatorade bottles are thrown. And the psychological composition of the team changes—what was once perfect chemistry of bodies and minds becomes a toxic, atomized mess."

Riley witnessed firsthand how those afflicted with the "disease of more" suffer from ego bloat, envy, a growing sense of entitlement, and alienation from other people.

In many ways, you and those around you are like that championship team—once a title is won or resources are created, striving for the best, the biggest, "the most" from your newfound situation is common. Ultimately, pursuing the elusive more can lead you into one of the most dangerous but unforeseen pitfalls of prosperity. And, it's one of the most common that people experience.

## Ethan's Acquisition of Things

After working hard for several years, Ethan successfully exited his business. He was pleased to discover that he was set up well financially, and he soon became entirely focused on the acquisition of "more." First, he bought the luxury car he had always dreamed of owning. Then he bought three more. His purchases escalated to a bigger house with more property, a vacation home, and another.

When he learned his friend had an exclusive golf membership, Ethan quickly secured his own.

While none of these things were bad in themselves, Ethan subconsciously chased the acquisition of things as a source of happiness. He kept seeking more and more, only to be surprised and saddened that, despite having all the money to buy whatever he wanted, none of these purchases brought the happiness he was looking for. Ethan owned more things than you could count but felt empty inside. He had prioritized things over relationships and was left alone and more depressed than he had anticipated.

It strikes me that this drive for "more" also causes the athletes Riley describes to become successful in the first place. This fierce competitive drive and ability to focus are significant strengths until they manifest as debilitating weaknesses. It's a common paradox—a high achiever's drive for "more" is their biggest asset until it becomes their biggest downfall. Like Ethan, it first brings great success, but then it leads to emptiness, and, once they start comparing themselves to others, even pain.

## The Comparison Dilemma

In the comparison game, these assets turn dangerous, putting you at risk of becoming infected with the "disease of more." This condition is particularly perilous because of how attractive more appears on the surface. Initially, when you have money, the ability to buy many things you've always wanted is exhilarating, and watching your dreams materialize is gratifying. However, this satisfaction is fleeting, as it soon becomes apparent that money is finite and cannot buy lasting happiness. The summit of Money Mountain becomes elusive because numbers and comparisons to others diminish your achievements no matter how high you climb. You will always lose because someone, somewhere, will always have a larger number than you. It's a peak you can never summit. It will always be just out of reach. Bailey, a successful business owner, notes this dilemma in her own life, stating,

> "I had a number that I was actively working towards, thinking, 'If I only made X amount of dollars, then I would be happy.' When I exited my business, I made far more than the number I had always dreamed about. In theory, I should've been ecstatic. But I wasn't. I was mad—jealous even—that my partner made it out with a bigger number than me."

Bailey was too caught up in the comparison game—her emotional health, happiness, and everything else was affected because she was stuck comparing her win to someone else's. The accomplishment of a lifelong dream wasn't a happy moment. Instead, she was mad. This is where people, even good-intentioned people, often fail. This dilemma of getting stuck on a number and attaching it to unattained happiness is a common theme I saw across our interviews.

This is the essence of the challenge of continuing to climb Money Mountain—it is inherently never-ending. True satisfaction and happiness come, not from the continual ascent, but from finding contentment and meaning along the journey.

Though that is sad, it's a fundamental aspect of human nature to desire a more prosperous, more abundant life. An insatiable desire to make more and have more was a consistent theme in my interviews. It's perfectly normal to view money as a solution; indeed, prosperity can be a source of real satisfaction once achieved. It's what we all work toward, and it's natural to believe that reaching a certain financial threshold will make all our problems disappear.

## The Will Smith Problem

---

Actor Will Smith recalls that when he was poor, he was depressed. He dreamed and hoped for the day when he would have enough money to make his problems vanish. However, once he achieved career and financial success, he realized his dream of money providing his happiness was an illusion. He had all the money he could ever want but found that it did not solve his problems. His hope that money would solve his problems had vanished, and he was still depressed, living a life full of challenges.

It is expected to buy into the notion that "all our problems would disappear if we had more." But when you possess more, you quickly realize that money cannot solve all your problems. This realization often comes painfully and swiftly. The Roman philosopher Seneca said, "For many men, the acquisition of wealth does not end their troubles; it only changes them."

This has proven true in my personal experience, the experiences of my interviewees, and many people I have met. Trying to solve problems with money is futile. You will never be satisfied if your sole focus is producing money to acquire things. Money comes with its own slew of problems and rarely provides real happiness.

## Chris's Wakeup Call

---

When his money came, Chris experienced a new problem in the form of an entitled son.

Chris always knew how to make money, and once he could buy whatever he wanted, he indulged in purchasing the nicest cars and toys. When money started flowing, he quickly focused on acquiring everything he had ever dreamed of. Over time, he amassed quite a collection. You name it; he had it—and probably several of "it." He was deeply infected with the disease of more.

It wasn't until this emphasis on "stuff" reflected back to him through his son that he realized he needed to make a stark change in his life. Chris's children grew up in affluence, and when they expressed a desire for something, they got it. When his son turned 16, Chris gifted him a brand new Jeep, which he customized to his son's liking. Although it was a generous gift, it only took a few months before his son began seeking a more expensive car to add to his collection. Alarmed by this development, Chris reevaluated his own collection of vehicles—many of which were seldom used—and realized he had set a detrimental example for his son. Deciding to make a drastic change, he sold his entire fleet. His son could not believe it. In dismay, he protested, "How could you sell all of your cars?" Chris responded,

### "They're just a piece of metal."

His son initially struggled to understand, but this marked the beginning of a significant shift in their relationship with material possessions. Chris's realization that he was perpetuating a cycle of superficial happiness led to a transformative moment. He recalibrated his son's perspective on life, shifting the focus from acquiring possessions to valuing more meaningful experiences and relationships. It required years of effort, but ultimately, Chris and his son reached a healthier understanding and found themselves in a better place.

While Chris's experience offers hope for recovery, it is challenging to combat this pervasive disease, as it is deeply ingrained in the human psyche to constantly seek more.

## The Hedonic Treadmill

In a study on happiness, psychologists asked many people to stop at random moments, rate their happiness on a scale from 1 to 10, and describe what was happening in their lives then. The respondents consistently reported a happiness level of 7, regardless of their activities or the time of day. Whether they were shopping for groceries, spending time with their family, working, or performing mundane chores, the rating was invariably a 7. Even during crises or exceptional events, they quickly returned to this baseline level of incomplete happiness.

The researchers were intrigued by this phenomenon. They concluded, "It appears that humans, irrespective of their circumstances, live in a state of mild but not fully satisfying happiness."

This constant level of happiness suggests an underlying dissatisfaction—a sense that true happiness remains out of reach. The elusive 10 on the happiness scale seems attainable if we only had just a little more, leading us to perpetually chase an unattainable level of satisfaction. This relentless pursuit is termed the "hedonic treadmill." Much like a hamster on a wheel, we continue to strive for a perfect 10, but we inevitably find ourselves back at 7. Despite occasional highs, sustained peak happiness remains elusive over time.

Though I recognize the dangers of the disease of more, I find that I, too, am susceptible to its temptation. I myself am infected. I know it, and it worries me a lot. It goes back to the two examples of my great-grandpa and my grandpa. I saw the effects of the illness happen first-hand in my grandpa's life. I know where his story ends, and I don't want you or me to suffer a similar fate.

Focusing solely on accumulating more money to solve problems is futile. Despite our best efforts, not all issues can be resolved this way. New challenges will continue to emerge, demanding our attention. So, as you try to make life more comfortable biologically, you will face a new set of diminishing returns. Recognizing this can reduce the temptation to chase after more as a solution to our perceived problems. As PayPal founder Peter Thiel wisely advises, "Before getting swept up in the competitions that define so much of life, ask yourself whether you even want the price they offer." In essence, when is enough, enough?

Ultimately, recognizing the pitfalls of the disease of more enables us to focus on what truly matters. It empowers us to lead more fulfilling lives, enriched not by the quantity of our possessions but by the quality of our relationships and the depth of our purpose and growth. When we accept that chasing more is not the answer, we are ready to consider what's next for us in our climb of life as we artfully avoid falling victim to the "disease of more."

# | 5 |

# Should You Stay, Or Should You Go?

I often get this question from business owners, founders, and working professionals: "How do you know when it's time to leave?" Though this is usually about leaving or selling your current company, it's a great reflection point for when to transition away from money as the focused output of your factory. The first step in finding your next peak is to step off the mountain.

Suppose you've already decided to leave Money Mountain and have exited your business, or you have transitioned away from your career or the pursuit of money. In that case, you can skip this chapter and move straight to navigating the emotions of leaving.

But for those still climbing, this chapter will help you decide when the right time is to get off and find your next peak. This juncture calls for a keen sense of timing and insight. This reflective pause is not just about where to go next but, crucially, when. Specifically, it helps you shift from the exhilaration of reaching new heights to the quiet introspection required to discern when it is time to seek new paths or step into roles that better reflect your evolved aspirations.

This moment will undoubtedly come when it's time to step off the mountain, but it can be challenging for many to recognize. Why? Because it is deeply personal, and in reality, if there isn't a reason to change, then there's no rush to (as this comes with its own set of challenges).

For those still working trying to figure out what they want to do, and if leaving is financially a realistic option, this simple framework helps in making this decision. There are three questions that make this decision pretty easy. If your answer is "no" to any or all three, then now may be the time to transition out:

## 1. Do you love what you do?

If you love what you do, why leave? Some fortunate individuals may have discovered a deep meaning in their factory with the focused output as money. They live up to the adage that you won't work a day in your life if you love what you do. For these individuals, there is still a purpose to be found in pursuing what they've done up until this point.

Kim, an architect, shares,

"I've decided never to retire. I love what I do; it's my passion and how I always want to spend my time."

For Kim, retooling her factory would rob her of something that would bring her lasting happiness. If she did transition away from her architecture firm, she would still do architecture for fun. So why leave the vehicle bringing her this much joy?

Think about aspects of your job that you love. Are these components something you can only find in this job, or could they be replicated or even enhanced in another role or venture? By exploring what you are passionate about and whether or not you find it where you're at, you'll find more profound clarity on whether now is the time to leave.

## 2. Do you love who you are doing it with?

If you are fortunate enough to work with a team that inspires, supports, and energizes you, leaving might have more negative implications than positive ones. Evaluate the dynamics of your current workplace. How do your colleagues and work environment impact your daily sense of well-being?

Ian, a business owner, could easily sell his company and walk away with a good deal of money that he could then use to retool his factory. His reason for staying? "I'm building extremely cool things with extremely cool people." Selling his business would be a huge loss for his friends and the thing that brings him much joy.

If you find deep fulfillment through your work relationships, staying alongside those who inspire you may make sense.

## 3. Are you doing good where you are at?

For some, their initial peak has opened up doors of opportunity to make meaningful changes in the lives of those around them, exactly where they are.

Take Tate, a CEO who could have left the business years ago. Tate chooses to stay at his company because he loves his employees and feels he can do more good for them in their lives if he stays than if he were to leave. He says that by staying,

"I can remain an advocate for the employees under me and create a positive work environment full of opportunities for those that I have come to love and trust."

If your role enables you to contribute positively to the community or make a difference in the lives of others, these factors are crucial to consider. If you're unsure, list how your current role allows you to benefit others. Does this impact align with your personal values and goals for making a difference? By looking outward, you may find that staying where you are makes the most sense.

Whether you choose to continue on your current path or decide it's time for a change, it's crucial to periodically reevaluate your motivations, the joy your work brings you, and the impact you have on others. This ongoing assessment helps ensure that your career continues to align with your evolving personal and professional aspirations.

If you choose to stay on the path that continues to output money primarily, you can still take the time to retool your factory to some degree. Regardless of whether you stay where you are or transition out, it's essential to reevaluate your time and approach to make sure that you maintain a clear purpose, have space for cultivating meaningful relationships, and create the attitude required to enjoy the journey.

But be careful if you decide to stay. When working towards great success, it can be easy to sideline other aspects of your life and difficult to focus on anything other than the pursuit of money. If you decide to stay, you may be conditioned to linger in old habits, and you could get caught up in the stress and minutia of the day-to-day business operations.

The good news is you can stay *and* enjoy your work. You can balance your life in a way that gives you time to focus on aspects of the business you want while also freeing up your time to experiment and find new ways to learn and grow inside your business. It also allows you to dig deep and determine how to make the biggest difference you can from the position you are in.

If you decide to leave, looking beyond Money Mountain and retooling your factory will be an adjustment. While it may be easier to kick old habits, you've likely grown accustomed to a particular way of operating, and it will require significant effort to reconfigure your life to produce something other than money. The way to it and through it will likely be uncomfortable and unknown. The following section will help you navigate these feelings and find yourself in a position to decide what your next peak will be. But first, dedicate the time and quiet introspection needed to find your deeply personal answer to the question: Should you stay, or should you go?

# | 6 |

# The Four Stages of
# What's Next

You naturally make a financial plan when preparing to step away from the phase of your life that brought you financial freedom. But you might not be prepared psychologically and emotionally for a very different existence. While many assume it's all rainbows and butterflies, it's a significant change that can cause distress and confusion.

While working for our company, I felt constantly weighed down by the incessant grind, risk, and pressure of being an entrepreneur. Though I enjoyed my time in the pursuit, I found myself ready to leave what brought me to this point of success. As I looked to get off Money Mountain, however, I reached uncharted territory that was difficult to comprehend and navigate. Until this point, I had measured success in terms of my career, but what did success look like when I prepared to leave all of that behind? I found this extremely daunting. Success was always intertwined with money, or at least to a certain degree. When I reached the success I had always worked toward, I considered how I would measure success if it were no longer tied to earning money.

Dr. Riley Moynes explored and surmised this overwhelming feeling. According to his research, you'll go through four stages after exiting a career or, in our case, transitioning away from Money Mountain. Understanding these four phases can help you navigate the transition and ultimately end up happy on the other side, ready to focus your factory on a new output. Successfully transitioning off Money Mountain is the first step in retooling your factory.

## Stage 1: Honeymoon

When you first enter the uncharted territory of a transition, it should feel like a honeymoon!

At first, it's an incredible feeling! You wake up when you want, you do what you want, and it's pure bliss. When an airline pilot first retired, he immediately bought what he calls his "Captain's House" and his "dream car"—a Camaro he had wanted since he was a teenager. He had wished to purchase both things his entire life, and now he had the means to accomplish his dreams. He was ecstatic! Like many in this situation, the pilot set out to enjoy his new stage of life immediately and bought his dream car and house. Suddenly, there are fewer obstacles to relaxing and pursuing your dreams.

While the instinct may be to purchase material possessions, try focusing on experiences. Time with loved ones is a massive component of enjoying the honeymoon phase. In all our interviews, this was the number one thing people pointed out as a positive result of money: being able to devote more focused time to family.

Enjoy this phase as long as you can. Have fun! Spend time with your family, go on trips, and have adventures. This is a time for you to enjoy the fruits of your labor.

Rachel, who's been through this stage, advises:

*"Take it slow. Celebrate and enjoy your success, but you will have this money for a long time, and there is plenty of time to buy new things. Go on a trip and spend quality time with family and friends. Take your family, and go live somewhere new. It will never get more convenient than right after you leave. Spend time exploring new places, trying new foods, and enjoying family time."*

Most people have a "bucket list"—a list of things they want to do that will somehow fulfill their lives. The phrase is best illustrated by the 2007 movie *The Bucket List*, in which Morgan Freeman and Jack Nicholson play men with terminal illnesses who try to live it up before they "kick the bucket." They go skydiving, fly over the North Pole, and ride motorbikes on the Great Wall of China, among other outlandish adventures. In the movie, one of the main characters is a billionaire and can afford to finance all the fun. The movie made popular the phrase *bucket list*, and millions made up their wish lists of things to do before they died.

It's fun and motivating to create and dream up a bucket list. However, when you've met your basic needs financially, the bucket list stops being a dream and could become a reality. You can realistically now tick off every item on your bucket list. But the bigger question is, what are the trade-offs?

The moment you can realistically achieve every item on your bucket list is when the bucket list could become a big problem. Strictly living for your bucket list is an imagined elixir. It's telling yourself that if you could just do, or have, or be this one thing, you would be happy. But what happens when you achieve that thing? Without the joy in the pursuit, the sad reality is that it doesn't provide the same fulfillment as it once did.

Brett decided that for his bucket list, he would go on every cruise offered by Viking—all fifty or so. He immediately set out to accomplish his goal when he could afford to. But after four cruises, he started to get nervous. "Is this really how I want to spend all my time?" he asked himself. What Brett thought would be his avenue to ultimate happiness turned out to be lukewarm at best. He was surprised that he felt sad and hollow as the cruises continued. What he thought would be relaxing and rewarding was incredibly lonely. What happens when your vacation extends so long that it becomes your life?

Over time, he discovered that he would rather be home with his family. It wasn't that the cruise in itself was a bad thing. But without it as a vehicle for a break or a reward in an otherwise busy and purposeful life, it proved a little empty in the experience.

Money can amplify your happiness as you use your newfound freedom to create memories and explore what the world offers. However, the double-edged sword of this phase is the lack of routine and purpose and the inner urge to be "doing something." The honeymoon phase won't last forever. For some people, it's only a few weeks; for others, it can last months or years—but it will end. Initially, you will love it, and you may not feel a care in the world. But eventually, you start to feel rudderless. You likely will experience extreme boredom, a lack of purpose, or even loss. When these feelings begin, you've entered the next stage.

## Stage 2: Loss

John, a business founder who retired at 40, said, "Having retired this summer and having enjoyed an extended vacation boating and relaxing with friends and family this fall, I was hit with depression about the loss of routine and purpose. I thought I was losing my mind as every one of my still-working friends kept saying how much they envied me. So my sadness compounded." Ironically, he envied them because they still had a clear purpose in their lives. This left him with a sense of emptiness, which denotes the second "exit stage": loss. It's the stage that all are aware may come, but hope never happens to them.

Many don't realize how emotionally expensive it can be to get off Money Mountain and retool their factory. Changing the inner workings of what has always been done is disruptive—it's almost as if it fries their brain. You've been needed for so long to provide and build, and it's emotionally jarring when you're suddenly not needed in the same way anymore. You're left feeling at a loss.

A similar phenomenon occurs when moms, having spent their children's entire lives nurturing and catering to their children's needs, suddenly find themselves empty nesters. No longer needed in the same capacity, it shakes their very identity to the core. One mom describes it like this, "I didn't know who I was anymore; I found myself wondering, what else was I good for? What could I find to be as fulfilling?"

This phase is paradoxical. You have achieved what so many dream about—the ability to do nothing. But you feel adrift, disoriented, and purposeless. You might even feel guilty that you have negative feelings toward what many people perceive as great. But negativity is typical. Your entire life, you've been outputting money in your factory. Now that that phase has come to a close, you need a new clear output.

During this stage, you might experience five different senses of loss:

## 1. Structure

You've had to wake up, work, and get a job done. Now, you don't, and losing that structure can be a big shock. One entrepreneur, Brent, spent his whole life going to work at the same time each morning and spending 14-hour days calling investors, negotiating with vendors, and generating buzz on social media for his product. When he exited, there were no more schedules or agendas and nobody to talk to. Brent was left with too much time on his hands and didn't know what to do with it. "I started reorganizing the house, which didn't last long. My wife told me I had to get out of the house because I was driving everyone at home crazy." He felt extremely bored and entirely alone. This is a common feeling I found across several of our interviews. The structure helped guide the interviewees' purpose; they felt extreme loss without it.

## 2. Identity

It's typical to identify with what you do every day. You were the person who was *doing* the job. You are now the person who *did* the job. While growing my business, I identified as, and took pride in being, "the Divvy guy." It was so universal that once, when I was out looking for my escaped dog, a neighbor, upon recognizing me, didn't say, "Oh, you're Alex," he said, "Oh, you're the Divvy Guy." That was my entire identity to him. It was tough for me to understand and internalize the change of identity once I was no longer the "Divvy guy."

I realized I wasn't alone in feeling this way as I dug deeper. Professor Arthur C. Brooks of Harvard says, "As a striver, I'm not going to lie, I'm afraid of becoming irrelevant. I'm afraid of losing the admiration of others; I'm afraid of failure; I just am."

President Ulysses S. Grant experienced similar feelings when he left the White House, writing, "I am now simply Ulysses S. Grant, and I am trying to get used to it." Few of us will face that big a change, but in a society where we identify by our work, losing that identity hurts and can leave us feeling unrooted and untethered.

## 3. Purpose

As we've discussed, it's natural to consider your purpose once you've reached financial security. You may wonder, what mountain should I climb next? Simon exited his business and was looking at living for another 30 years. He described his feelings on his new-found retirement as follows:

"Thirty years of vacation isn't a dream; it's a nightmare."

He continues, "Living a life with no purpose other than to play golf or tennis every day and eat out every night gets old fast. I can't tell you the number of times that a friend has told me how bored they are with retirement."

Purpose is like a good physical workout—it's tough, but the recovery and long-term results feel amazing. The endorphins, the adrenaline, that healthy high you get from exercising, you can't buy; you have to do the workout to earn these results. Lack of a challenge leads to apathy. With nothing to "earn," life becomes gray and meaningless.

An acquaintance of mine left college early to backpack Europe solo for six months. He set out with high optimism and excitement for new adventures. He came home after three months, halfway through his intended time, because the lack of purpose was so powerful that it sent him into a deep depression. He shares, "I was surprised how quickly not contributing to society in a meaningful way started to wear on me. It didn't take long before I wondered what I was doing out there." A sense of purpose is crucial to finding lasting happiness. Without it, one's feelings of extreme loss only compound.

## 4. Relationships

Relationships are an important topic that I discuss in their own dedicated section later in the book, but it is important to touch on them here. Despite your best intentions, you may find that your business partners, employees, clients, and friends start to fade out of your life. Many of these are treasured relationships, but with the everyday connection gone, it's hard to stay in touch.

Of course, you can get together for lunch with your friends from work, but as Moynes says, "It doesn't take long for you to realize that you're a fifth wheel, that you're no longer part of that group, and that they have moved on."

Additionally, it can be hard to relate to others outside of your workgroup if you're not in the daily grind. Like my friend chasing entertainment through various hobbies, he inadvertently distanced himself from all his friends who still spent most of their time working. They no longer had common ground to relate to or merit regular conversation. Without these meaningful interactions, he was left feeling lonely and isolated. Even finding people who are willing to listen can be challenging. One entrepreneur became a multimillionaire at a young age. Her dad told her, "You don't know how your friends will look at you, so don't discuss it with them." She was disappointed to discover he was right—her friends' attitudes toward her were bewildering. None of them had the patience to listen to what was going on in her life. She felt like she couldn't talk to them about anything. Even her mom got bitter, saying, "You're going to have so much more money than your dad and I combined, and we've worked all our lives for it." Many of our interviews described the same phenomena of strained relationships and changed dynamics when exiting Money Mountain.

> "Be careful when selling your company because when you do, you'll just become a guy in a corner."

Becoming less important to everyone around you can make you feel like you've lost your impact. Most of us want to leave behind a legacy—a memory of our impact on the world—so we will spend some time later investigating how to do just that.

The loss stage is the most challenging phase and can be incredibly lonely. The intensity of loss and guilt that comes with money can shock you. The good news is that, in time, you'll move to the next phase. It will just take some trial and error.

## Stage 3: Experimentation

Just as you had to experiment as you started your career to find where you best fit and what brought you the most purpose, now is the time to experiment and "write your second act." Experiment with where you want to spend your time and money in the long term.

Jeff explains, "When I first exited my company, I started interviewing people who sold their companies 10–20 years ago. One of them advised me to leave the house every day and be gone for a full workday. Whether you have something to do or not, find an office space and leave. You and your family need to see you leaving the house, and it will push you to try new things."

Jeff added that his kids needed to know what Dad did all day. If his answer were "nothing," it would set a terrible precedent for what he wanted his kids to do in the future. A person who does nothing stands for nothing, and he didn't want his children to think that was acceptable.

It's time for trial and error, and you might make many errors. Thomas Edison conducted hundreds of failed experiments, but he said, "Negative results are just what I want. They're just as valuable to me as positive results. I can never find the thing that does the job best until I find the ones that don't." You might write a book, join company boards, or find a way to serve the community. These are great ideas that work for some people. Others go entirely different directions and start a new business, spend time developing talents, or fund a charity. This experimentation phase is a personal journey and can be exciting! Find what works best for you, but recognize that in the end, to be happy, you do have to find a deep purpose.

So, how do you know if you have a purpose? The answer falls along the lines of what we started discussing at the beginning of this section. Ask yourself:

*Am I actively creating something of worth?*

*Am I in pursuit of an "unconquerable" challenge?*

*Do I feel like I've earned my sleep when my head hits the pillow each night?*

If you can easily respond to these questions in the affirmative, you probably have a purpose, which is great! It's no small thing to have something to actively work towards. However, if you do *not have a new, concentrated purpose,* you may wonder, how do I find one? To start, try to explore your "deferred dreams." What have you always dreamed of doing but needed more time or resources to accomplish? Maybe you'll rediscover some old passions you put aside while climbing your way to financial security. There's a reason self-actualization is at the top of Maslow's hierarchy of needs —realizing your dreams and continuing to grow in fulfilling your potential leads to you being true to yourself and achieving inner peace. Self-improvement works wonders for your health as well. A recent study shows that a treatment process that seeks self-actualization reduces death, anxiety, and depression in patients. By pursuing self-actualization through finding meaning and happiness in life, individuals lead themselves toward positive well-being.

It's important to remember that simply exploring hobbies is not the same as finding a deep purpose. As I recounted, shortly after leaving my company, I decided to take piano lessons as part of my time meandering on Hobby Hill. While I loved doing it, I didn't have any musical goals, and it became just a way to stay busy, ultimately leading nowhere. That's the difference between meandering around and finding a meaningful purpose. One business owner offers a unique strategy to lead experimentation: asking those closest to him.

*"I was the CEO forever, then suddenly, I wasn't. It hit me pretty hard and put me into a weird place emotionally. I started reading and talking to people about how to recalibrate. I interviewed some friends and asked them why they were friends with me. It was awkward, but it helped me see what I was good at and where to spend my time and talents. I [would] recommend that anyone needing to redefine themselves go through that process."*

It won't be easy to experiment with your life, and it can sound daunting, but you need to keep trying different things until you discover what makes it so you want to get up in the morning and hit the ground running. If you don't, you could easily fall back into stage two, loss, where no one wants to be. It's the road to nowhere and the road to unhappiness. Like many retirees who spend the rest of their days in front of the television, it's often an empty and purposeless existence. "Men who have attached their sense of identity and value to their work can become depressed in retirement if they can't successfully transfer that attachment to new interests," reports psychologist Dr. Alan Berman, an expert on why men commit suicide. Dr. Moynes says that of all the retirees he's observed, "The toughest to watch are those who remain in or slide back into Phase Two." It was incredibly sad for him to see these individuals suffer so much.

## Stage 4: Reinvention

"Not everyone breaks through to stage 4," says Dr. Moynes, "but those who do are some of the happiest people I have ever met." Reinventing yourself can be the most satisfying part of becoming financially independent. But it can also be the most scary. Though you may be afraid, this is not a good reason to stay where you are. While success at this stage looks different for everyone, it almost always comes from serving others.

In this stage, you are going to recover the five losses of phase two:

1. **Structure:** A reinvented life means a restructured life. With a compelling new mission, you will naturally develop new routines and establishments.
2. **Identity:** You may have become what you always wanted

a compelling new mission, you will naturally develop new routines and establishments.

2. **Identity:** You may have become what you always wanted to be—an author, painter, philanthropist, craftsman, teacher, local politician, etc. You've cemented yourself in a new identity of what you attack each day.

3. **Purpose:** Climbing your second mountain becomes just as important, or even more important, to you than climbing the first one.

4. **Relationships:** Though old partnerships may fade, you connect more deeply and meaningfully with family and new friends.

5. **Impact:** You can still be an influencer in your circle, and with the energy of your new mission, that circle of influence can grow beyond your imagination.

A prime example of reinventing yourself post-financial success is Grant. As a young man, Grant had become aware of the legal challenges that face abused and battered women. Lauren, his wife, who was already an attorney, was equally motivated to help those most at risk, so together, they started their own firm.

"We can now spend our lives helping women who don't have the resources to help themselves. We want to be defenders of these vulnerable women, and I don't need their money." People said to him, "But you're 47 years old now. You'll be 50 when you get out of law school!" His answer: "So? I'll be 50 whether I go to law school or not!"

This had a compounding effect on his community, himself, and his wife. By not having money as the focus of his output and by re-inventing himself as a lawyer who helped abused women, he built an incredible Factory for Good.

There is no magic bullet for preventing the disorientation and dislocation of your factory reconfiguration, but knowing this four-fold cycle of emotions will help you navigate and eventually reach a good place. You can anticipate a more fulfilling future on the other side of this cycle. Wherever you are on this journey, genuinely enjoy the honeymoon of phase one, prepare for the feelings of loss you will experience in phase two, experiment and try as many different things as you can in phase three, and find real fulfillment in phase four. As you navigate these emotions it is helpful to recognize that though it may be difficult, we each have to conquer the four stages of what's next.

# | 7 |

# The Happiness Audit

When you've successfully navigated the four transition stages, you're ready to move on to the next step: reconfiguring your factory. You're ready to embark on your next peak. You may have a clear picture of what to do next with your life, but that picture might not seem so evident when that day comes and you start on your path. You might feel paralyzed as you face the decision: what *will* you do with the years ahead?

We've covered what to avoid doing and how to work through some of the emotions with leaving, but what tactile strategies can help you determine what will make you happy? As you consider "what now," it is helpful to define the things that are most important to you as best you can—the things that give you the most happiness, joy, and satisfaction. The idea is to passively reflect and actively engage with your desires and aspirations, mapping them out as clearly as you map out business strategies.

On a business trip to New York, I found myself on a plane, daydreaming about what I'd do when I exited. Looking out the window across the empty sky, I imagined the day when I would finally have the resources to do whatever I wanted to make me happy. This got me thinking: *will the money actually make me happier?*

I decided to write down all the things that made me happy and rank them in a "Happiness Audit." I assigned a value (how happy it made me on a scale of 1-7), a cost to each item on my list, and the duration of how long each thing stayed with me. I fully expected to identify what on my list I could do more once I had more money at hand. Here's a sample of what I wrote down:

*Figure 7-1: The Happiness Audit*

| SOURCE | VALUE | DURATION | COST |
|---|---|---|---|
| My spouse | 7 | Long | Priceless |
| Eating good food | 5 | Medium | $$ |
| Throwing a ball with my son | 7 | Long | Priceless |
| Family dinners | 6 | Long | Priceless |
| Golfing with friends | 5 | Short | $$$ |
| Spending time outdoors | 5 | Long | Priceless |
| Playing the piano | 4 | Short | $ |
| Scrolling social media | 2 | Short | $ |

I was surprised to discover that most of what I wrote down, with the highest rankings on both value and duration, didn't cost a lot. In fact, most of them cost literally nothing. What I had assumed would be a ticket to greater happiness had no bearing on how I wanted to spend my time to make me happy. The "Happiness Audit" tool provided a snapshot of my values and illuminated the discrepancies between what I thought would make me happy and what actually did. Quantifying happiness this way was enlightening—revealing that the simplest pleasures often yielded the highest returns regarding contentment and long-term satisfaction.

This realization echoed a powerful lesson a friend had taught me years earlier about the true source of happiness.

As I started building my business, I asked him, "But what if I'm unsuccessful?" This is a real fear for most of us, especially those setting out to build something of their own. His response was simple: "If you have all the money in the world, you vacation in Hawaii. If you can't afford Hawaii, you vacation in California. If you can't afford California, you'll go camping." His point is that there's a common denominator: spending time with loved ones, the part that makes you happy, was a constant. It doesn't matter where you are or how much you make. Ultimately, money doesn't play a significant role in determining your happiness.

The exercise I completed on the plane and my friend's advice changed my perspective on what makes me happy and helped me reorient my life toward what matters to me. When I exited, I revisited my spreadsheet, and I still find the Happiness Audit a valuable tool in finding a deeper purpose as I look to retool my factory. It is a helpful exercise to complete periodically at various stages of life—a simple check-in of who you are at your core and what makes you truly happy. In short, it can be the root of what gives you the strongest sense of purpose and the start of discovering what your next mountain will be.

Viktor Frankl, the esteemed Austrian psychologist, observed, "Everyone has his own specific vocation or mission in life...Therein he cannot be replaced, nor can his life be repeated; thus, everyone's task is unique as his specific opportunity to implement it."

This perspective emphasizes that your mission should capture your unique contribution to the world, leveraging your strengths and passions.

As you review the results of your Happiness Audit, consider: What does your happiness audit tell you about what you should live for? What did you value most in your audit? What brings you the most joy? What is worth spending your resources on? Find a quiet place and probe your heart and mind to find the answers to these questions.

This introspection is a powerful tool that clearly defines what you live for. It helps you focus on your pathway to the future, choose the goals that matter to you, and bypass the "fatal distractions" that can keep you from achieving your great purpose. Whether you use it as a periodic check in, or as the basis for your decision to decide your next peak, it's always a good idea to look to the Happiness Audit.

# | 8 |

# Living Life in Crescendo

Retooling your factory into a Factory for Good is an incredible opportunity to hit your second wind and, as Stephen R. Covey famously said, "Live life in crescendo!"

To a musician, crescendo means gradually swelling in passion and volume. It comes from the Italian verb *crescere*—to grow. To you who are planning a life, it means "a progressive increase in intensity"—an upsurge in energy, a growing sense of contribution, influence, meaning, and enjoyment. Living in crescendo means not wasting away your life doing things that don't have a meaningful, overarching purpose behind them. As we've explored, aimless living eventually leads to a permanent sense of loss. Stephen R. Covey also said, "the best way to predict your future is to create it."

After graduating from Harvard Business School at twenty-five, Covey decided on his overarching purpose: "I want to unleash human potential!" That was his driving desire and his clear mission statement for decades. He fundamentally believed everyone had the makings of greatness if only they could unlock their latent capacity. He made his mission actionable, and as a teacher and writer, every book he wrote and every lecture he gave advanced that aim.

The publication of *The 7 Habits of Highly Effective People* made him rich and famous. Some 40 million copies have been sold. It became so popular that it transformed everyday language—terms like "win-win," "proactive," and "synergy" entered common vernacular. The book found its way to the desk of every business and civic leader in the world. But even after making this huge impact, Covey didn't go into "diminuendo" mode (the musician's word for quieting down, backing off, "diminishing"). For him, living in crescendo was a mindset, a principle of action. "It redefines success," he said, "from how society usually measures it." It means not resting on your past contributions but considering that you might still make meaningful contributions. Covey continued to speak, write, and live his mission for years to come, even until his death.

Living in crescendo means continuously improving your mental, spiritual, emotional, and physical health. It means intentionally nourishing your spirit through service worship or the arts instead of mindlessly starving yourself of the higher things in life. It means investing in loving relationships instead of locking yourself behind emotional gates and becoming a psychological recluse.

Above all, crescendo means having a mission that heightens and intensifies your love of life.

## The Transformation of Tangelo Park

Harris Rosen, a successful Florida hotel chain manager, exemplifies how taking action can help you live in crescendo. In his fifties, he was invited to speak to the elementary school students in Tangelo Park, an impoverished suburb of Orlando.

"How many of you are planning to attend college?" he asked. He watched in dismay as only two or three hands went up. "That has to change," he said, making it his mission to implement the changes he wanted to see in the school.

First, he set a goal that by the time college admission applications came along, he would have set up a way to provide a scholarship to any student in Tangelo who graduated from high school—which he accomplished. This generosity took the town by storm as word spread from the older high school students to the younger grades.

When he asked the same elementary students the same question a year later, every hand went up. But the scholarships were only a start for Rosen.

He evolved his mission to target the next generation of students by making childcare available to every child. He put his arms around the whole community of Tangelo, funding free daycare centers and preschools, and fought to have these resources available for every child in need.

Before Rosen came on the scene, Tangelo was fighting a war against drugs, crime, and endemic poverty. Only half of the young people even attended school. Now, a couple of decades later, property values have climbed. Houses and lawns are welcoming. Crime has plummeted.

Recently, 40 of the 45-member high school class graduated with Rosen scholarships. No other school in Florida can boast a 90 percent college-bound graduation rate. Why the fantastic transformation of a struggling community into a showplace? "We gave them hope."

Rosen says: "Why devote countless hours to school if college, with its high cost, is out of reach? If you don't have any hope, then what's the point?"

Rosen's mission was to help a discouraged community find hope and escape poverty. He had a clear mission to change the lack of aspiration he was seeing in elementary-aged students. He translated that mission into tangible, practical goals that made a measurable difference in many lives. In Harris Rosen's case, he found that offering a scholarship to each graduating student in Tangelo was the strategy that paid off the most in terms of achieving his goal. Rosen's scholarships were not just a generous gift, but a strategic intervention that addressed the root cause of educational disengagement in Tangelo Park. By ensuring financial support, Rosen effectively removed the primary barrier to higher education, which resulted in increased student motivation and college attendance rates. Though he couldn't control whether or not a student graduated, he could control the giving of scholarships, which he did in a way that influenced the entire community.

## A Mission to Empower the Unemployed

A Cincinnati couple likewise took action after deciding on a second peak. After reading about the plight of the unemployed in the Cincinnati area, Taylor and Shannon (a couple who had sold their own business) decided to volunteer at the local Job Service; this state agency helps people find jobs. It was a frustrating experience.

Their goal was to find stable employment for each person who came to the agency, but most people they tried to place in jobs didn't stay in their positions longer than a few days or weeks. They would beat the bushes to secure a job for a single mom, and she would go to work, but within a few weeks, she would be back in line for an unemployment check. This happened so often that the couple was about to give up.

Then they heard about a thing called the "90-Day Rule." Most attrition happens within the first three months on the job, but if employees can hold a job for three months, they are much more likely to stay with it. There are all kinds of reasons for "quick quits." A single mom has a sick child, has to stay home, and loses her job.

Or they miss a bus and fail to show up. Or they need more experience with a manager. Whatever the reason, the majority leave their jobs within the first ninety days. So, Taylor and Shannon searched for the right strategy to keep their clients on the job for at least three months. They tried out lots of ideas, such as providing daycare and transportation services. These things helped, but they didn't get the desired results.

One day, they read in the *Wall Street Journal* that one major industrial company was improving employee retention by assigning each new hire a "buddy" whose task was to help that person get oriented, build up skills, make friends, and solve problems like childcare and transit. This buddy system made a big difference in keeping the new hires on the job.

Shannon and Taylor got this program going with several of the big employers around the city. The program was the strategic lever they had been looking for. Soon, nine out of ten of their clients were sticking with the job for the "magic" three months, after which they were used to the routines and had found their place. They became stable, productive employees, many staying for years and changing their financial circumstances entirely.

This couple met their goal beautifully once they had found the right strategy. It involved research and lots of trial and error, but their mission was achievable once they started pushing on the right lever. With a clear focus on what makes you happy, and with your values incorporated into an actionable mission statement, you will have a clear purpose that you can use to fulfill your life.

While you may think that living in a crescendo sounds intense, Beethoven shows us that "slowing down" does not mean you can't live your life in a "crescendo" (the Ninth Symphony is loud toward the end!). It does mean that you focus more on the lasting contribution you make to the world's happiness at whatever pace you feel the most comfortable. And this pace can change!

Armed with the knowledge of what makes you truly happy and understanding the pitfalls that may keep you from climbing your next peak, you're ready to live your life with purpose, making the unique contribution only you can make. Conquering the first pillar, Purpose, is an integral component of establishing a factory for happiness (i.e., Good). This metaphorical engine does not drive us toward more money, accolades, or leisure but toward more meaningful contributions to our loved ones, our community, and the world. It's about leveraging our resources, including money, to create lasting happiness through positive impacts rather than continuous consumption. If done successfully, it is the epitome of living life in crescendo.

# RELATIONSHIPS

"Love and relationships enrich life in ways that money never can."

**- ANONYMOUS**

# | 9 |

# The Only Thing That Really Matters

On a podcast with a fellow athlete, Shaquille O'Neal reflected on his life and career. During the conversation, he encouraged other athletes to spend time with their families and loved ones, admitting deep disappointment that he hadn't. Instead, he had focused on other things, like fame and fortune. He didn't emphasize his relationships, which led him to live a life he regrets. He honestly admitted, "I'm in a 100,000-square-foot house by myself." Hurt by his decisions and where he placed his values, Shaq is now encouraging others to focus on what he, in hindsight, recognizes as really mattering: relationships.

In 1938, Harvard University began a project called the "Harvard Study of Adult Development." The project continues today, involving some 1,300 individuals from hundreds of families. Researchers periodically check on the study subjects, asking them about their health, finances, families, and friends. They've watched as generations of people are born and grow up, find families, fall in and out of love, succeed and fail in business, and die. It's the longest-lasting, most ambitious longitudinal academic study ever done. So what can the researchers say after all these years? The study "has brought us to a simple and profound conclusion." They say, "good relationships lead to health and happiness. The trick is that those relationships must be nurtured."

I think we can all recognize and agree with this. Of course, we want to nurture the relationships that matter in our lives. So why, then, is this harder in practice to accomplish? Why, despite our best efforts, do relationships fail? This is a broader question that could merit a book of its own, but I am specifically interested in the connection between money and its effect on relationships—both positive and negative.

In some cases, money has the potential to amplify relationships. I saw this with my great-grandfather as he placed a priority on using his resources to create memories with his family and friends and focused on giving back to his community. However, it is a genuine thing that money can ruin relationships. I saw this with my grandfather. Though he had two marriages and several children, he unintentionally ended up severing ties with most of his relations and was abandoned and alone at the end of his life.

While we all likely aspire to use money to enhance our relationships, the unfortunate reality is that money's ability to ruin relationships is very evident across the board. If you're not careful, you can, and will, lose what is most important to you.

Although money can ease financial stresses on marriage, the wealthiest Americans have a roughly fifty percent divorce rate, which aligns with the average rate among the general population. Also, according to the American Academy of Matrimonial Lawyers, "the more you earn, the more trouble can brew between a couple … Overall, divorces tend to pick up, rather than decrease, in periods of economic growth, when incomes rise." As for the well-being of children, the picture is mixed. The good news is that higher net worth leads to fewer familial behavioral problems. The bad news? More and more children of wealth creators are showing up in psychiatrists' offices. One child psychiatrist reports, "The kids I see are given all kinds of material advantages, "yet they feel that they have nothing genuine to anchor their lives to. They lack spontaneity, creativity, enthusiasm, and most disturbingly, the capacity for pleasure." This trend has multiplied since the early 2000s. Clayton Christensen once said, "There is no evidence that business success will make us happy people or allow us to have happy families."

He saw this pattern as his Harvard MBA experience meant that Clayton went to school with many who became notable in business and found financial success. This is what he noticed about those people:

> *"Over the years, as I've watched the fates of my HBS classmates unfold, I've seen more and more of them come to reunions unhappy, divorced, and alienated from their children. I can guarantee you that not a single one of them graduated with the deliberate strategy of getting divorced and raising children who would become estranged from them. And yet, a shocking number of them implemented that strategy. The reason? They didn't keep the purpose of their lives front and center as they decided how to spend their time, talents, and energy."*

In other words, despite their prominence and prosperity, Clayton's classmates failed to navigate their affluence intentionally and ultimately lost out on what was most important.

## Carl's Late-Life Realization

After enduring a troubled childhood where he never felt he was enough, Carl spent his entire life building and creating, trying to prove that he *was* good enough for others and himself. After years of working hard, he had several successful exits and experienced significant financial success. In his mind, he had done it—had proven his worth—and he should have been happy. But he wasn't. It took him until age 56 to realize how unhappy he was. He looked hard at his life and realized that he had no real relationships, was unmarried, and was estranged from family and friends. He decided to turn to a life coach for support. For the first time, Carl wondered if there was something else he could do that would bring him joy.

After working with the life coach, he identified a clear action plan to look outward and develop meaningful relationships. He started to spend his time in service to others, volunteer at local charities, and be engaged in his community. In serving others and building relationships through those service activities, this man was able to get rid of the mental cages he had, telling himself he had something to prove, and a year later, he was much happier with several meaningful relationships in his life.

Carl realized later in life that his relationships and happiness were directly affected by his decisions about how he spent his time, effort, and money. And it's not just our close relationships that matter—entire generations are at stake.

## The Johnson Family

In the nineteenth century, a young pharmacist named Robert Wood Johnson and his brothers started a company by making and selling surgical instruments. The company they founded is now worth billions and has become a household name and brand for selling Tylenol, Bandaids, and Listerine. I'm sure you know it; it's called Johnson & Johnson. The company is, of course, a storied success; the Johnson family, however, not so much.

Massive wealth had an objectively negative effect on Johnson's welfare. Satisfaction with their billions evaded them. They were always looking for more—more cool cars, elaborate mansions, exciting adventures, gold and jewels, and glamorous spouses—and for some, it became too much.

One Johnson son began using drugs in his teens and became famous for wrecking exotic cars. High on LSD, he once drove a brand-new BMW onto a beach. While he got out to exhilarate in the view of the sunset, the car disappeared in a rising ocean tide. In his twenties, he died of a cocaine overdose. His brother, also a drug abuser, was well-known as a reckless motorcyclist. Within days of his brother's death, he died himself in a high-speed crash. He had just received his trust fund check for $10 million.

The adverse effects of money continued to the next generation. One of the Johnson grandsons became a playboy, jettisoning his second wife at age 76 to marry the housekeeper, who was 34. He built her a 54,000-square-foot mansion on 170 acres and left her his vast fortune—igniting a battle among his six children over the will.

The chaos was yet again passed down to the next generation—one of his sons led a fraught life involving attempted suicide, a bizarre shootout, and a long fight over the paternity of his children. A fellow heir built an underground road from his house to the street; it turned out to be 300 yards long, with a special entrance to his personal barbershop. This kind of mounting extravagance has accompanied an increasing number of broken marriages, attempted suicides, drug deaths, and conflicts over several generations.

Now, I recognize that the Johnson and Johnson family story is extreme; their extravagance and chaos are on a whole other level.

However, through the extreme, we can see money's negative effect on generational relationships. Actual relationships and the health of individuals—both mental and physical—are at stake.

To compound the tragedy, money doesn't seem to last beyond the third generation. The Williams Group performed a 20-year study of 3,200 families and found that 70% of wealthy families lose their resources by the second generation, and a stunning 90% lose them by the third generation. That means relationships suffer for something that is largely fleeting. This leads me to consider—is it worth it? There are pitfalls tied to prosperity, and it can be difficult to navigate them.

## Prioritizing What Matters

So, what should you do to safeguard your most valued relationships, especially when prosperity reigns? Once you have yourself centered around a clear purpose, it's time to focus on nurturing your closest relationships.

Many people realize this lesson the closer to death they get. Psychiatrist Richard Friedman writes about a beloved colleague, a trauma surgeon, who found herself dying of lung cancer. She still had months, maybe a couple of years, to live. "She felt physically fine—vital even. That's why I was so surprised when she said she had no desire to spend whatever time she had left on exotic travel or other new adventures."

Instead, she wanted her husband, friends, family, dinner parties, and the great outdoors. "I just want more Long Island sunsets. I don't need Bali," she said. She did not want to trade her time with loved ones and the home she loved for novelty and excitement. In short, she prioritized her closest relationships. Dr. Friedman observes that this is a common pattern with people approaching the end of life. They don't want to trade away what really matters to them for trips or crazy adventures.

We can learn a lot from their example. As we invest ourselves in those things that matter, we can make a "list for living"—a list of things we can do with our resources that will build solid relationships and contribute to the world's happiness.

As this will be your partner in every aspect of life, start by focusing on your spouse or significant other. For many, this relationship is the only thing that really matters.

# | 10 |

# Protecting Your Marriage in Prosperity

Consider your relationships as three circles, with you at the center. Circle A, closest to the center, is your closest relationship, usually your partner and/or children. Circle B extends to other family and close friends, and Circle C entails your community.

For many of us, our spouse, partner, or significant other falls within this inner Circle A. You'll want to do everything possible to protect those relationships at all costs. This becomes especially important as we consider money an amplifying force in a relationship—it can very realistically cause it to thrive or fail. Whatever your Circle A relationship is, if you ruin it, your entire life is at risk of being flipped upside down. Regardless of the amount of money, comfort, or resources you have, it won't matter. Money won't be able to protect you if things get crazy with your significant other or kids.

I saw the danger of this in my own life. Though I would say that my wife and I are in a great relationship, the exit really tested us. It caused us to have probably the most challenging year of our marriage in over 15 years. Some of it came down to how we were raised and how we reacted so differently to this change in our lives.

My wife, Megan, grew up in a single-parent household. Her parents divorced when she was young, and her mom, now single, incredibly raised six kids on a small salary for most of my wife's life. As such, there was little money to go around. Purchases were carefully planned for. Recycling and upcycling were important. Necessities took priority in their home, and Megan's mom instilled a thoroughly frugal mindset in Megan and her siblings.

So when the exit came, and we suddenly had access to money, it was genuinely hard for her to change her mindset. Due to her childhood background, she had difficulty justifying purchases and grew increasingly concerned that we may inadvertently ruin our children by spoiling them. This stressed her out so much that at one point, she would reluctantly admit that if she could, she would've pressed the "Easy Button" to go back to the way life had been because she was overwhelmed in trying to figure out what her new life would look like and manage the changes that were occurring.

I, on the other hand, was raised in a different financial situation. So when the money came, I found it easier to adapt and was more eager to change our lifestyle to prioritize nice things for our family. Disagreements quickly arose when the subject of money came up.

Over time, we realized that we disagreed on how to proceed with daily purchases and long-term planning. We had to reconsider everything regarding our family's established mode of financial operation up to that point. It was all new territory.

In confronting this new terrain, we had to decide how to give, save, and even talk about finances. We both were determined to value our marriage above everything else and ensure it survived the pitfalls associated with money. While there is no single way to do it right, we knew we wanted to get on the same page again. So, over time, and with a lot of give and take, we have become comfortable regarding money in our relationship. I know it sounds ridiculous, but it was much more complicated than we had ever anticipated. We were constantly surprised, but this was actually the most challenging year of our marriage.

In conducting my interviews, I discovered that I wasn't alone in money introducing some difficulty into my Circle A relationship. While many know that a mutually agreed upon financial plan is requisite for any marriage, an *emotional* financial plan is also vital to help you navigate the emotional complexities around money. A mutually agreed upon emotional financial plan is rarely smooth but essential. Misalignment in priorities of how to spend money can cause tension and stress or a rift between both parties in a relationship or a marriage. It happens all the time.

One man I interviewed, Eric, tells the story of his parents, who grew up in East Germany when it was a socialist state. Early in their marriage, they were entirely devoted to each other and "got along fine," he says. Few people had any money in the communist world, and his parents were no different, but careful savings, stretching, and reusing got them through.

When Eric was five, the Berlin Wall came down, and East Germany plunged into capitalism. Eric's dad founded a company and soon got rich by his neighbors' standards. They enjoyed this newfound wealth, bought a "Western" car, remodeled the kitchen, and quickly built a prosperous enterprise.

But that's when things "went sour," Eric says.

*The problem was that my mom was not prepared for more money in the same way my father was. She had always had a frugal lifestyle and had no idea how to change that. She didn't enjoy shopping; she hated it because she thought it was showing off, and she feared alienating her friends. She would refuse to buy anything new and hold onto her things, like her old pots and pans, until they fell apart.*

*My dad would offer to get her new things, but she always refused, saying that what she had was good enough. After a while, my dad got tired of her rejection and started buying new stuff, which only made her resentful. The chasm between them deepened. I doubt they even realized what was happening.*

When Eric was twenty, his parents split up. They never found any ground for agreement. Different mindsets about money and a lack of communication can destroy a marriage.

Take my family history as an example. My great-grandfather cherished his relationship with my great-grandmother. Together, they raised a beautiful family and took time to make sure their relationship was strong and thriving. My grandpa, on the other hand, didn't put time and effort into his first marriage, and it ended in divorce. When he married someone much younger than himself several years later, money became the most important part of their relationship, and she ultimately chose money over him.

It's easy to point out relationship problems but harder to execute strategies that help protect and cultivate a partnership. In my marriage, we discovered that a transition event mandated that we align and ensure we were on the same page going forward in our new normal. While there's no "quick fix" single answer, here are some strategies from our interviews on what other people are doing to minimize conflict in a relationship affected by money.

**Strategy #1 – Work on the Relationship**

Somebody once said, "The main thing to remember is that most matters concerning money in a relationship are not about money at all." The real question is, how sturdy is the foundation of trust and love on which you've built your marriage? Discuss together what your relationship requires to keep this foundation solid. This could be therapy, a regular date night, or a couples retreat. The key is to continue doing simple things for your spouse that demonstrate love and trust.

Even the most emotionally mature partners can disagree sharply about money. Work on conflicts by listening carefully to each other and ensuring you understand where your partner is coming from. People who feel understood tend to feel less conflicted. Suppose conflict does arise, and you can't resolve it together. In that case, it is helpful to call on a trusted advisor, someone you know who has the wisdom and neutrality to act as an intermediary to help you find solutions.

## Strategy #2 – Have "Money Meetings" Regularly and Often

Fabian and his wife, Luisa, realized that they seemed to never be on the same page when dealing with money. It would inevitably come up at inconvenient times and usually end in an argument. After months of frustration, they dedicated one hour weekly to discussing money topics in a safe space to have these difficult conversations.

Fabian shares, "It was incredible. We were able to share how we were each feeling about our spending, parenting, and communication about money. Conflicts happened less often and were quickly resolved. We were able to reference decisions already made in our money meetings and easily get back on the same page."

Ideally, both partners should be on top of how they feel about their money—and this is independent of the amount of money a family may have at their disposal. It's always good to have both members of a partnership understand the current pulse of their financial status and, more importantly, how they are navigating the emotional side of money in their lives. In these meetings, you can discuss:

- How are we feeling about where our money is going?
- Are we still aligned on our financial goals?
- Is there any major parenting decision we need to consider related to financial literacy?

Wise couples put their heads together more than once a year. More frequent meetings are even better because you will feel more secure about the financial plan's progress. You can help keep each other accountable for your goals.

**Strategy #3 – Avoid Adopting a "God Complex"**

Upon reaching financial success, Eli was annoyed when he saw an uptick in conflict with his wife. When he confronted her about it, she pointed out, and rightfully so, that he was surrounded by people who always said "yes" to him. She said, "Your employees, advisors, and often friends always say yes, only I say no." He realized that this was the source of their conflict. He was humbled and made a conscious effort not to let everyone around him turn into his "yes men."

Though I hate to say it, money talks. Like Eli, paying to be right always becomes possible, even if done unconsciously. This can lead to a God Complex or inflated feelings of infallibility. Many successful executives begin to think they are the center of the universe. This becomes an issue in your relationship, where you will disagree some-times. And, if your significant other is the only one saying "no" to you, this will cause some tension. I've seen time and time again this God Complex adopted by peers, and rather than work to remove it from their relationship, they look for who will say yes to them, trading affairs for dissension and ultimately destroying their mar-riage. By looking outward and avoiding adopting this God Complex, you'll be better able to safeguard your marriage.

As you find balance in your partnership, even with prosperity, you can place a higher priority on what matters: your relationship.

Alignment in your relationship is essential and becomes even more crucial when considering tackling the pitfalls of prosperity with kids in the picture. Being on the same page and the same team is critical when parenting your children, who likely also fall within your Circle A relationships. Now is the time to be intentional with parenting your kids to help them navigate their emotions around their finances. This can be very difficult, and was listed in our interviews as one of the hardest things to navigate; second only to protecting your marriage in prosperity.

# The Bank of Mom and Dad

There was a small town located in the middle of the desert. This town was like any other small town in every way except one. In the town square, there was a single ATM. This machine was unlike any other ATM—it was magical. When a townsperson used this ATM, it didn't show their balance or ask questions about their credentials. It simply spit out money. Sometimes, it gave whatever amount was requested by the townsperson, and sometimes, the townsperson was denied. But it was consistent and never tied back to a balance. The townspeople didn't have to work; they just went to the magical ATM and hoped for the best. They were confident that it would provide for their needs.

The ATM was reliable and never incentivized work or independence. While this was, in many ways, nice, people in the town never learned how to manage money. They became lazy, entitled people and could never leave town as they were always tied to the lifeline that was their magical ATM.

While this story is obviously fictitious, it is the reality for most parents. You, the parents, are the ATM to your "townspeople" (your children). How many times do your kids come to you and ask for money? How often do you say no? If you think about it, your relationship resembles a magical ATM. This phenomenon was so common in our interviews that we've coined this relationship between children and parents as the *Bank of Mom and Dad.*

Of course, as a parent, you provide for them when they're small, but as they grow—if you're wise—you'll gradually move into a relationship that mirrors that of a banker instead of a benefactor. Remember the magical ATM—the townsperson who got money every time they went to the ATM without constraint never saw a need to work, budget, or understand the value of money. Of course we all want to avoid a similar outcome when it comes to our kids.

It's almost inevitable that your kids will think of you as a bank. Children look to their parents to provide for and support them. Poor expectations and habits can lead to an unhealthy dependency that is in danger of continuing in our kids, even as they grow to be adults.

It's not anyone's fault, but it is the responsibility of the parent to raise their children in a way that leaves them financially responsible. If they knowingly or unknowingly look to you as a bank anyway, then some constraints should be in place that protect your relationships with your kids and act as a great tool in their financial literacy.

## Danger in the Gray

Let's talk about Travis and Emma's situation. They had parents who were very generous in their gift-giving. Emma's parents gave Emma and Travis a brand-new Toyota for their wedding. When it was time to purchase a home, they loaned them the down payment for a house. The terms of the loan? "Just pay back that original amount, no interest." No payback schedule and no due dates. Nothing like "pay us back in five or six years." They just said, "When you can." They made similar loans to all of Emma's siblings. Used to their parents' free, easy financing, Travis began to notice that his wife's siblings had no intention of paying them back. Confused, he approached his in-laws and asked, "This is a loan, right?" They responded, "Yes, it's a loan, but you can pay it back whenever you feel you can." After that, they never asked about it. Travis felt he should pay them back, and he did, but he thought that the siblings interpreted their" loans" as gifts and was alone in paying his in-laws back.

Because of this experience, Travis established a more defined "banking" style relationship when loaning out his money. He clearly outlines when the payment is due, the interest rate, when the loan matures, and any other relevant details. He wants to make sure everything is clear. "I want them to feel like they have to do something for the money."

Travis's experience perfectly exemplifies why a family banking relationship needs to be carefully thought through and clearly articulated. If it's not written down, there is danger in the gray. If expectations lie in a gray area, a relationship could likely be ruined.

As I have talked to people, *every* parent is a bank to their kids, but hardly anyone I know operates from a charter or a set of rules. Without clear-cut terms, things become ambiguous around money, and ambiguity is dangerous, especially when investments and money are involved. When life tells us no, the parenting is done. When there are things in life you can't have because of circumstances outside of your control, no further action is required because not having the thing you want is simply a natural consequence of life circumstances. However, parenting becomes a necessity when the ATM occasionally gives money freely while other times, it refrains.

Steve, a successful lawyer in Virginia, bought homes for all his children. He recognized how hard the market was making it to get into a house; he loved his children, and he wanted to keep them close. They were reasonable homes at a reasonable price. When home values skyrocketed, one of the children decided to sell the house and use the proceeds to move across the country to Colorado. "Wait a minute," Steve said. "That's my house, bought with my money— shouldn't I have a say?" And the kid argued, "No, it's not. What are you talking about? It's in my name. "

Well, whose house is it?

This dynamic is the result of unclear expectations.

Julia told me one of the toughest stories I heard in all my interviews, highlighting the dangers of unclear expectations:

*As we earned more income and the kids got older, we paid for all the simple things—their clothes, a car, and activities. When our daughter went to college, we paid tuition, room, and board. Honestly, we didn't think anything of it.*

*But then her spending habits changed, and her bills got bigger. We were enabling her spending, paying for an extra year and a half of college. When she got married, we were excited—at last, she'd be on her own. But it didn't work out that way. She would still text us, and we'd cover the rent for a few months, but then it was a few more months. We thought it'd get better, it'd get better, but we kept having to open the checkbook. Finally, there was a divorce.*

*She moved back in with us, and we covered more schooling so she could change her career. But it went on and on for several years. Eventually, we realized she had a behavior problem, not an asset problem, and we cut her off with a couple of months of living expenses. No more opening the checkbook. I thought we were very reasonable—she was thirty years old, she would go out and get a job, pay her rent, and it would all make sense. But what happened? She blew up at us.*

*There is no longer any relationship. Now she says she hates us, that we don't love her, and that she will never talk to us again. She posts on social media how mad she is at us. But I've heard from my son, her brother, that she is gaining confidence in herself and paying her rent for the first time in her life. She's realizing that she can do it without us. Of course, we're hoping she'll come around and we'll have a relationship again, but we're worried that might not happen.*

*Quite literally, the lack of a contract or financial structure got us into this situation. Nothing was written down regarding our financial relationship with her, so we can empathize with her feelings. The ATM was always giving her money, and suddenly, it wouldn't give her anymore. It was the "gray area" that killed us—the absence of a clear understanding of our responsibility and hers.*

How sad is that? These parents provided everything for their daughter and did what they thought was best at the time. Money is why they no longer have a relationship with their daughter. I look to that story as my own worst nightmare, as I'm sure most parents would. We all want meaningful relationships with our children and will do almost anything to avoid every scenario that risks our relationship.

In addition to putting your relationship with your children at risk, consider that undefined and unrealistic expectations might damage the character of your family members. Their core attributes and the type of person they become may also be at risk.

## Jenny's Downfall

Jenny grew up dependent on her parents for financial support. They bought a house for her and her husband. The idea was that Jenny and her husband would pay rent to the parents, but when they reneged on that agreement, there were no consequences. When Jenny's marriage got rough, they divorced, and her parents have continued to cover all her expenses. Unaccustomed to being self-reliant and used to nice things, Jenny consistently takes advantage of this kindness, even when she wants to indulge herself in extravagance. Jenny's parents are at a loss. Jenny has developed a behavior problem, not an asset problem, and they're trying to figure out how to move forward.

We are all creatures of habit. When we make a habit of depending on the help of others, we start planning our lives around that help. If we take responsibility for the choices of our family members, we deprive them of the chance to become responsible for themselves.

In this light, the purpose of the Bank of Mom and Dad extends beyond distributing wealth to teaching family members how to keep commitments. It becomes an instrument for developing responsibility in your children, and its value lies in the discipline it provides. Children learn to make and keep promises, which helps them avoid debilitating dependence. Parents learn how to raise independent kids and how to set clear boundaries.

## How to Setup Your Own Bank of Mom and Dad

1. **Create a charter for your bank that is based on your family's mission statement.** What commitments have you already made as a family? What do they imply for the use of the family's resources? For example, your family mission might contain a statement of where you will invest your joint resources. That mission should govern the bank. You probably already have a "bank charter" of sorts. It's usually not written down, but it defines how your family handles money. "In our family, we always splurge at Christmas." "I believe in counting every penny and entering it into a ledger." "If my kids need a hundred or less for something, I don't worry about it—I just hand it out." My point is that your family culture for handling money already exists. But it might not be intentional, it might not be what you want it to be, and you might be damaging your relationships and the character of your family without a definite plan. Regarding family finances, renowned business consulting firm EisnerAmper says, "The creation of a written family charter is an important step toward ensuring that the family and the family business are aware of the rules that will guide what can be expected from each. Even the simplest charter can successfully inform, reassure, and guide everyone who has an active interest in the success of the family business and a vested interest in keeping the family at peace."

2. **Decide who will be held accountable under the bank terms.** It might just be you and your partner and your children, or you could include your parents and siblings and their families. Going beyond that can get complicated, but

regardless, it is important to set some boundaries on who will be held accountable under the bank's terms.

3. **Stay strong with your terms.** The family bank will fail if you start "forgetting" or being flexible about the terms of a loan. What's worse, relationships will fail—not only the relationships with the defaulter but also the relationships with other family members who honor their terms. For example, you may have one brother who pays back the loan while another one doesn't. This can create conflict between all three of you. In setting the terms, ensure you don't make them harsher than you're willing to enforce. This way, you can stay consistent, and the Bank of Mom and Dad can remain effective.

4. **Remember that you are not just making loans—you are helping your family members succeed.** Family members typically ask for loans for higher education, mortgages, or business startups. Your family bank exists to enable the growth and development of those you love the most, so their success will naturally be your top priority. Still, the definition of success will vary. One family bank lent a young couple, who was just starting out, enough money to buy a nice piano. The couple didn't need a piano in the sense that it would feed or house or clothe them, but the young husband, a fine pianist, loved playing, and few things helped him and his wife destress more than the music. In later years, they used the piano to teach their children, who grew up with a wealth of musical talent. Was the loan for a piano a "practical" investment? Probably not, but the dividends in family relationships, personal satisfaction, and development were considerable. Not all returns on investment are financial, and in a family bank situation, successful people count more than profits.

5. **Consider using a third party as your family bank advisor.** You might want that trusted advisor to administer the charter and make the decisions. This provides a clear advantage to a third party that can be the "bad guy" and hold people accountable. This can make it so that you aren't the one potentially ruining the relationship and can always have someone else to whom you can deflect. With that professional in the mix, your family members will be more thoughtful about the requests they make to the family bank. When managing the family bank, preserving the family itself is the goal. Just as a wise banker puts the community's success first, a wise family banker prioritizes the thriving of the whole family. If that's your core value, then the family bank can unite the family rather than divide it.

## The Martin Family Bank

The Martin parents had made considerable money in real estate. There were five adult children, four daughters, and a son, along with sons-in-law and one daughter-in-law. A close and loving family, they decided together to invest their funds for their family's future.

They made one significant acquisition—a property next to an interstate highway that was rural, undeveloped, and uninviting. No trees, no water, no actual use. It was not suitable for farming or grazing. But the Martins' son, an attorney and trained commercial real estate investor, saw the potential of a hub development due to a nearby highway interchange. The closest population center was gradually expanding in the direction of this property, so the son believed the property would pay off eventually. Until then, the property demanded much attention. It produced no revenue, so property taxes were burdensome. There were constant legal and zoning issues. Water rights had to be negotiated.

Under the family bank, each first generation had an equal vote in all major decisions. They kept meticulous records. They met as a board of directors on a pre-set schedule. Requests for loans were carefully considered as children needed money for college, business startups, down payments on houses, or emergencies.

This family bank successfully governed all their decisions for over forty years, even after the parents passed. The Martin grandchildren grew into careers and families, built homes, and paid off their debts to the bank. Eventually, the property anchored a significant new office park, the investment paid off, and the whole family came out handsomely.

But beyond the financial success of the family bank, the Martins grew closer to each other. What could have been loosely defined had been tightly defined. Family members learned the importance of keeping their commitments to the family. The family could have been ripped apart over ill-defined expectations and slack financial discipline, creating resentments or embarrassments; instead, the children and grandchildren grew up within a culture of integrity. The Martin family bank did more than govern the Martins' money; it helped create a happy family of mature contributors to society.

And that is what the Bank of Mom and Dad is about. It's about raising our kids in a way that helps them when the time comes to launch out of your home and go out on their own. There's much conversation to be had at that time regarding who's paying for rent, school, books, lodging, transportation, and food, and an established bank or plan can help you navigate all of it.

The Bank of Mom and Dad can become an entity that protects your children and helps them grow the financial independence you desire.

## Sophie's Close Call

Sophie is a prime example of how to use a family bank to help an at-risk daughter whose spending was out of control.

Here is Sophie's story in her own words:

*I have three kids: two in college and a daughter in high school. The other day, I realized how close I came to ruining my daughter's life.*

*A few years ago, her dad, my husband, developed a life-threatening illness. He knew he had only so much time left, so we got distracted from our daughter's life. We compensated by giving her a lot of presents and saying yes to everything she asked for. I gave her access to my Amazon account and one of my credit cards. We had some fun trips and elaborate dinners and did lots of shopping without thinking of the ramifications or consequences to my daughter's character.*

*When my husband passed away, it took me a year to get out of the grieving stage and realize that I had hurt my daughter. As I started to look at her credit card transactions, I was shocked. She had slipped into a lifestyle that she could never replicate on her own. I knew that if I didn't interfere quickly, she would grow an entitlement mentality, and would be entirely dependent on me.*

*I spoke to her about disciplining her spending. She didn't understand me, and when I cut the credit card up, it was like taking a drug away from a user. I ultimately had to change my cards and passwords as she found workarounds to access my funds. She had no sense of the value of money. Going through this withdrawal was traumatic for her.*

*It took me about a year, but I sat with her repeatedly to hammer out a contract she could live by. The terms were specific: I would pay for certain things like school and gas for the car, but she would have to pay for dates, fun, food, and extras. Budgeting was a new concept for her. The contract enabled her to see just how much she would need to contribute to the family budget. We wrote these things down on paper so we would know exactly where the money was coming from and what I was willing to support. Writing it down gave us a framework for making decisions in the future.*

*To keep up her side of the agreement, she agreed to get a job and volunteer on Saturdays at a local shelter. She needed to understand the value of work and service. Through this exposure, she learned the power of turning outward. And she's in a completely new place regarding living a life she can replicate on her own when it's time to leave the house.*

Sophie discovered two critical benefits of a "Bank of Mom" relationship. First, kids need to know how the bank is going to work. They need to know that it will not be an ATM where they can withdraw whatever they feel like. They need to understand what Mom and Dad will pay for and what they will not pay for. While there is no single correct answer, the boundaries you set can gradually make that entitlement mentality disappear. The important thing is that there needs to be clear boundaries.

Second, the parents also develop a discipline, a framework for decision-making about money. They embrace the parent relationship instead of acting only as a deep well of cash that will never be accounted for. Because parents' opinions differ, a family bank helps them to get on the same page and stay there. In my case, I would pay for some things my wife would not pay for. Until we write down our expectations together, our children will go from one parent to another, like from one ATM to another. A clear plan won't prevent this from happening every time, but it will make it a lot less likely.

As you help protect your children from the pitfalls of prosperity, it becomes crucial to establish the Bank of Mom and Dad.

# | 12 |

# The Spending Agreement

Everyone wants their kids to be independent and to become positive contributors to society. And the family bank is a great way to help rear children who can be 100 percent self-reliant. Yet I discovered many examples of people doing everything that contributes to their kids being the exact opposite of what we want them to be. Why is this?

Life teaches about money—it has a way of saying no. But when you have resources at your disposal, life no longer says no. Why say no to new clothes, expensive trips, or a new smartphone? It is no longer because you can't afford it. Now that life is no longer the teacher of financial responsibility, the parent has to be the teacher. Though, this is much easier said than done.

Once, as an experiment, I got a group of people together to find out how they were handling the challenge of raising their children, as it pertains to establishing the Bank of Mom and Dad. I simulated the quiz show "The Newlywed Game" by asking them to write separately how they would handle certain situations. I went through about eight scenarios. For example,

*"Your ten-year-old wants dance lessons. It's expensive, but she wants it. Will you pay for 0%, 25%, 50%, 75%, or 100%?"*

*"Your twelve-year-old asks to go to a movie with friends."*

*"Your fifteen-year-old gets invited to a birthday party and needs a present."*

*"Your nineteen-year-old graduated from high school but still lives at home—will they pay rent?"*

As we followed "The Newlywed Game" format, it became clear that with young kids, parents would pay for everything. But as they thought about their kids getting older, they started to diverge about what they would pay for. As they discussed, emotions began to fray. "I want that older child to pay rent," one partner would say for example, while the other said no. The big issue was how to raise children toward a world where they would be responsible for themselves and at what age that responsibility would take effect.

It was interesting to hear these conversations. The couples generally thought they were on the same page. They were sharp, intelligent, good parents making good homes, yet essential differences of opinion began to surface. They left the game thinking, "We've got to have this conversation. We've got to write down the rules to our family bank because we are not remotely on the same page as we thought." Far too often, the parents just let things happen organically. They're not even having these conversations or writing down their conclusions.

Put yourself in this game for a minute. Your thirteen-year-old daughter comes to you, "Hey, I want to go to a movie with my friends tomorrow. Can I have some money?" Will you pay for all of it, some of it, or will you split it in half? Now, ask your partner their answer and make sure it aligns. This is a simple question, but the answer will already be spelled out if you have a plan in place. It will specify what the child will pay for at what age. If the bank charter says she has to earn the money to go out with her friends, then she will already know the answer. The fact that she has a clear understanding of the rules makes parenting easier. Instead, she might ask, "Dad, how could I earn more money to pay for things like this?" That is a much healthier conversation for you to have with your children and for your children to have with themselves. It's a spending agreement between you and your children, allowing everyone to be on the same page. It prevents the kids from approaching each parent separately, hoping that "the ATM" says yes when the other parent says no. After simulating "The Newlywed Game," we decided to chart some of the responses as an example of what a spending agreement may look like. This diagram shows that the parents pay for most expenses while the kids are under twelve. However, as each child reaches their teenage years, the parents begin to wean themselves off of paying for everything. The breakdown gets less and less until a child is entirely dependent.

*Figure 12-1: The Spending Agreement*

| | Education | Rent | Insurance | Car | Food | Clothes | Fun |
|---|---|---|---|---|---|---|---|
| <8yrs | ● | ● | ● | ● | ● | ● | ● |
| 8-12yrs | ● | ● | ● | ● | ● | ◑ | ◗ |
| 13-15yrs | ● | ● | ● | ● | ● | ◗ | ◐ |
| 16-17yrs | ● | ● | ◑ | ◗ | ● | ◐ | |
| 18-22yrs | ● | ◗ | ◗ | ◐ | | | |
| >25yrs | | | | | | | |

## Starting Financial Literacy Early (ages 8-15)

Even though you naturally pay for most things when children are young, you can still prepare them for later life by teaching them core principles.

Experts discuss three principles to teach children even when they are small: patience, autonomy, and responsibility. Delayed gratification teaches patience, earning money teaches responsibility, and making choices about how to use money teaches autonomy.

**Example #1 – Patience**

Teaching kids to wait until they earn whatever they are asking for can help our kids appreciate it more and decide if they want to spend money on this or that shiny object. We helped our daughter learn this lesson when she asked for a smartphone. Everyone else at school had one, and she was always begging for one. My wife, being financially conservative, continually said no. Finally, she made a deal with our daughter: you can get a phone if you finish a larger goal: something meaningful to the family. The whining stopped. My daughter immediately and dutifully worked towards this larger goal. It was a long process. It took her over six months, and she probably put in over fifty hours to reach her goal. When she accomplished it, she felt she "earned" her smartphone. And we were able to teach her a lesson in patience. It was a win-win, and we felt it was the one thing we'd done right in parenting.

### Example #2 – Responsibility

Kids need to understand, and take responsibility for, the value of money at an early age, even if she isn't yet old enough to have a job. This became apparent in Stacy's life. When they went back-to-school shopping, her daughter wanted everything. After arguing about it, Stacy and her daughter agreed to a set back-to-school budget. Now, with the budget front and center, her daughter, who previously wanted everything, began to put things away and make the right decisions on how to spend her allowance. She took responsibility for how to spend the money she had available.

### Example #3 – Autonomy

Allowing your children to earn money themselves gives them a sense of autonomy. Another friend agreed to finance a 3D printer for his son on condition that the boy would produce 3D printouts to sell. He started making money and was able to pay his dad back for the printer and make a profit. When he stopped using it, he had to face the reality that he worked hard to get it, and it helped him make future decisions about buying things. If his dad had just bought it, he would've just asked again for the next thing and moved on quickly because it's easy come, easy go. Kids will spend their own money much more frugally than yours.

Patience, autonomy, and financial responsibility are core and can be taught at a very young age. The opportunity for teaching grows as children get older. You have the increased opportunity to start conversing with them about saving and spending, the power of compound interest, and the difference between paying it and earning it. You can even show them simple graphs of the exponential curve in the value of savings over time and how much they sacrifice if they *don't* save or explain to them the concept of net worth as a measure of financial success. By simply including your children in financial conversations, you can prepare them at a young age for what's to come.

Take opportunities to instill in your children basic principles of money management from the time they are little. Remember that "little kids have little problems, big kids have big problems." If you deal well with the little problems, you'll minimize the big problems later on. It's never too early—or too late—to start. Be intentional about it. Schedule regular and frequent visits with your children to teach them basic finance principles. Don't expect them to "pick up along the way" the wisdom to handle difficult circumstances. This involves teaching them how to make good decisions about money.

## Teaching Through Big Ticket Items (ages 16-17)

The opportunities to teach our children about finances increase the older they get, especially when they hit the magic age of sixteen. Without a game plan, it can feel overwhelming when kids finally age into the marketplace of cars and other big-ticket items. But if carefully planned for, this can turn into a phenomenal teaching opportunity. If you manage your kids' expectations well in advance, they won't have any reason to assume you'll be happy to make big outlays for them. You can successfully avoid causing any conflict or ultimately teaching your kids nothing. Let me illustrate what I mean.

When Mark's kids turned sixteen, he gave them each a new car. He wanted to showcase his success and do something nice. His oldest wanted a Suburban to cart all his friends around; another got a Jeep Grand Cherokee to go off-roading; and the third child, Sarah, chose a brand-new Porsche. She was used to getting the best of the best.

A few months after receiving the car, Sarah drove her Porsche super fast and earned a bunch of speeding tickets. Her attitude was, "If I crash it, I'll just get a new one." While this was never explicitly said, it was implied by how easily she got the first one. After months of reckless driving, she did end up crashing the car. Unapologetically, she asked her dad for a new vehicle. At that point, Mark realized he had made a big mistake. Though his first two children made more logical choices in their vehicle types, none of the kids had any skin in the game. They had developed an entitlement mentality with no accountability for the family's resources. Mark rectified the situation, working with Sarah to buy a beat-up Corolla she had to help pay for. With skin in the game, it was a much different and better experience for both of them.

Throughout my interviews, I heard stories of families with interesting approaches to handling large purchases, and they work! Here are a few of my favorites:

## Example #1 – Make it a Shared Experience

Kevin shared a unique approach involving purchasing an old, broken-down car for under $2k. He invested the money but approached his son, saying, "This car is yours, but you have to work with me to put it back to an operable state." Kevin and his son spent countless weekends and evenings fixing the old car. When they were done, Kevin gifted his son the car as promised. Even though Kevin made a small investment, the time spent with his son was priceless.

## Example #2 – Incentivize Investing

Samuel and Lydia set out to use the purchase of a car to teach some basics of finance. As their son Liam turned sixteen, they said, "All right, this is what we will do. We think you're a great kid. We're excited for you to have a car. Now, here's the budget. We're going to give you $10,000. It won't be enough to buy a new car; it will be a used car. But we also want you to see the $10,000 as an opportunity. We will double as a gift any money you don't use to buy the car, and we can invest it together. So, if you put in $7,000 to buy a car, we will take the remaining $3,000 and add another $3,000. You will have $6,000 in investments that you could use to pay for college or other life expenses." As Liam thought about it, he got excited about how much money he could make in investments and went off to shop for a decent car for as little money as possible.

After carefully researching and weighing his options, he returned and said, "Okay, I've found a car that will work for $5,000. So, can you take the other five and put it into investments?"   Samuel and Lydia bought the car, invested the remaining $5,000, and doubled it to ten. Liam bought the car at sixteen and is now twenty-three. That $10,000 has multiplied four times. Not only has it been a financial addition to his life, but it's also been an impactful lesson. He learned about the power of investment *and* depreciation—the unpleasant fact that cars don't hold their value. These parents were wise enough to know they were not buying a car, they were raising a financially intelligent son.

**Example #3 – The Family Dealership**

The Blacksmith family took a unique approach to car purchases. Again, the aim was to use cars to teach the kids how to be productive with money. They set up a "family dealership" with several vehicles in the family "fleet." They sat down with their two teenage kids (both had after-school jobs and could afford to pay some for a car) and showed them how automobiles are financed, including not only the purchase price but also the costs of insurance, fuel, and maintenance. They then explained how the use of vehicles was going to work in their family.

It went like this: "Okay, here's how it's going to work. Dad and I are the owners of the dealership. You can access the family "fleet" by paying us $250 monthly. Now, the cars are not yours; they're ours. You're more than welcome to drive a car to a date or a dance as long as you keep it clean and treat it with respect. We'll pay all the expenses. Remember: If you cause any damage to the cars, your monthly payment will go up to cover repairs." By treating the arrangement like an actual lease, the parents taught the kids financial responsibility and encouraged safety and vehicle care. They had skin in the game and knew they would pay a price if they didn't keep up their end of the bargain.

### Example #4 – Buy the Beater

Kati decided that when her children needed a car, she would help them buy one but only buy a cheaper, reliable vehicle. Kati's daughter, upon reaching 16, asked to buy a car. Kati asked her how she was going to pay for it. She replied, "If it's my money, I'll buy a beater, but if it's your money, I'll buy a nice one." After some discussion, they decided to buy the "beater" so she would have more money for other things. This demonstrates how large purchases are also an opportunity to teach kids about depreciation and amortization. Show them how quickly some purchases, like new cars, lose value while other investments, like real estate, tend to gain value.

### Example #5 – Loan Your Car

Several people I interviewed bought a car or used an old car from the family as a loaner vehicle for kids in school. They let the kids borrow the car whenever they needed it, and it was essentially theirs to use. The kids were responsible for gas and any other related expenses that came as they used it, but as the ownership was in the parents' names, the parents paid for the insurance. When the kids were done going to school, they were given a choice to buy the car from their parents or return the loaner for the next child to use or for their parents to sell. The key here is that the car belonged to the parents. There were rules and responsibilities attached to their child using it. The child never felt entitled to something because it was explicitly never theirs.

There is not one size fits all when it comes to large purchases. What works for one family won't necessarily work for another family. Whether you buy a car for your child or just a portion of it for a monthly payment, or you cover only gas and insurance, make sure your child has some financial stake in the game. Remember, you are raising responsible people, not just buying cars for them.

## Fighting the Failure to Launch (ages 18+)

One of the biggest milestones I encountered in our "Newlywed Game" was when children graduate from childhood and enter the world of adulthood. For many, this means moving out of mom and dad's house and going to college. This is a—if not the—pivotal moment to teach financial lessons in a way that cultivates independence and allows them to be self-sufficient, contributing members of society.

To illustrate what I mean, let me share Dave's experience.

Dave was a very successful business owner with a large family. He wanted to provide all of his children with opportunities that he didn't have growing up and decided to send all four of his children to college, with all expenses paid, for as long as they wanted. In his mind, they would go to college, graduate with a respectable degree, get a job, and become financially independent, as he had done many years prior. Without this expectation set, however, he was dismayed to find that none of his children had any interest in a life their father did not fund. His oldest, now thirty, with three degrees under her belt, has yet to get a job. She's returning to school for her second doctorate rather than trying to use her education to find a job and earn her keep.

His son got caught up in the social life of college, only took part-time courses, and is now in year six of pursuing his first degree. Another daughter, overwhelmed in her first semester living on campus, chose a school within commuting distance from her parents' house. She moved back in and only leaves the house when necessary for classes. His youngest is just starting school, but with the examples of his older siblings already in motion, he has begun to follow suit, pursuing expensive "exploratory" semesters abroad and lacking any real direction in what to pursue.

Dave finds himself frustrated by continuing to pay their expenses. He does not want to go back on his bargain and is finding it difficult to navigate. He continues to fund his children's education but wishes constantly that they would learn financial independence.

Dave's experience is a common one. Every parent must wrestle with the degree to which they will fund their children's education and the gray area of what to pay for when a child moves out of the house. Of course, we want what's best for our children, and, especially without the natural and highly valid excuse of "we can't afford it," we may find it difficult to discern how much is too much when funding our children's education.

I've collected some of the best examples across my interviews of how to navigate this successfully and gracefully.

Note that there isn't a one-size-fits-all solution to this predicament. These are all examples of navigating large purchases and using them as a teaching opportunity to help raise financially responsible children. Ultimately, you need to find the best approach for you and your family, but hopefully, these examples help illustrate the importance of being intentional when children move out.

By providing clear financial parameters and a supportive environment for your college-age kids, you can help them develop a productive mindset for transitioning into adulthood.

## Example #1 – Give a No-Interest Loan

Benjamin had the money to pay for all of his children's education. A firm believer in the value of education, he decided to pay the way in full to any child who chose to go to college. However, he made it a loan from himself to his children. While he didn't charge any interest, he did expect the full payment back after his children had worked a few years in their respective careers. To hold his children accountable, he had papers written with an agreed-upon term length and amount for his loan. Each of his children could attend college and pay their dad back in full according to their agreed-upon terms. They not only learned the minutia of loans, but also were able to feel ownership over their education as they paid their dad back in full.

## Example #2 – Set a Budget

Austin carefully planned to pay for his children's education. But, wanting to make sure that he was equitable to all of his children, regardless of where they chose to go to school, he set an equal budget for each of his children. He explained to them, "I have allocated this amount of money for your education. It will pay for school in full in-state, but if you choose to go out of state or to a more expensive school, this is all you will get." This contributed immensely to his children's education but left them deciding whether to work or take out loans to go to a more expensive school or where the school was entirely covered. Each of his kids made their decisions and went to their respective universities. They were grateful for what was donated, but understood that it was finite. They also learned the importance of a budget.

## Example #3 – Tuition and Rent Subsidy

The Browns set clear expectations with their daughter, who was off to college. "We'll pay your tuition and rent, but the rest is on you." While they cover living costs and education, their daughter works full-time to pay for food, books, clothes, fun, and a car. After four years, the tuition and rent subsidy will disappear, and she will be alone. It's all written down and transparent. The Browns could afford to pay for more, but they see their real goal as helping their daughter become independent and self-reliant. They want the next four years to be for a college education and an education in financial literacy.

So far, they're seeing her become more mature. She doesn't whine or complain about more money all the time. Instead, she stays grounded and works hard. She knows her parents are contributing a lot, but she also knows there's a time limit on that contribution. Many of her classmates' parents pay for everything without boundaries or time stamps, and the incentive is wrong. Her friends think, "I'll stay in school as long as possible." With this daughter, the incentive is the opposite—she is encouraged to move efficiently through school and get to a position where she can provide for herself.

## Example #4 – Incentivize Them

Jared was required to pay for college himself and found it a formative experience in his life. So, when it was time for his children to go to college, and although he could financially afford to pay for their way, he decided to use their college experience as an opportunity for his children to learn financial literacy and to earn their education. When each of his children graduated high school, he explained, "You're on your own for school. If you need a loan for housing, classes, or whatever, I'll loan you the money, and although I won't charge any interest, you have to pay me back the full amount within a year." He offered to loan them money to help them avoid student loans and the debt that would hang around their necks. This still allowed Jared to feel like he could support his children while teaching them. He explained further that to incentivize them away from taking out this loan, "For every scholarship you get, I'll pay you a percentage of the scholarship value in cash." This encouraged his children to avoid taking out loans, apply themselves in school, and ultimately get scholarships to fund their way through college. Many of his children, not wanting to take out a loan from Dad, or upon having taken out a loan and wanting to pay him back within the year timeframe, worked jobs while attending school. But their incentive was to, first and foremost, do well in school, earn as many scholarships as possible, and get through quickly. Although it was hard for Jared to hold this boundary, especially when his children were upset he wouldn't help fund their education further, he has found that, ultimately, this strategy was successful. His children graduated from college with high marks and avoided taking out student loans. They are now in careers of their choice, completely financially independent from Jared.

## Example #5 – Establish a Set Credit Line

Carol tells her kids in their senior year of high school that she will not just pay for everything when they go to college. "I will give you a lump sum from the family business into a bank account. From that, you can pay your tuition and living expenses. Essentially, it's a credit line that is yours to spend as you would like, but that's all you'll get from the business. That's your inheritance for the rest of your life."Her philosophy is that once they know it's not their mom's money anymore, it's theirs, that they will think about money differently. They'll be a lot less likely to throw it around and more likely to use it wisely. Whenever a child requests funds from the credit line, she tells them, "It's your opportunity to be an adult and decide what you will do with your inheritance. You're going to go to school and spend it wisely. If you're smart, you're going to save most of it. So, what do you think? Are you going to invest it, or are you going to, you know, go squander it?" In this way, she puts a lot of responsibility in their hands early on.

One daughter recognized this quickly, exclaiming, "Oh my gosh...this is for everything—like my education, a car, my wedding, potentially a down payment on a house?" Carol answered, "Yes, this is it, and it is all you will get. It's a lot of money, but there is nothing else."Fortunately, Carol's daughter started to take actual ownership of the money. She thought hard about where to go to school, how to get through quickly, which classes to take, and so forth. Carol's approach is intended to help her children avoid burning through money thoughtlessly because "Mom's paying for it." When the money is yours, and you've got your skin in the game, you tend to mature quickly. Carol made it clear to her daughter that she had an incredible opportunity but could blow it all if she didn't do it right.

These are just a few examples of other parents' actions, but you have to find what works best for you. The important thing is to discuss this with your partner and children and come up with a strategy that works well for your family. If left undiscussed and undecided, that is when there is danger in the gray, and relationships are put at risk.

Ideally, the lessons from the above strategies will inspire you to choose one or come up with your own as you get on the same page about raising financially independent children. However, money has an emotional side that will affect your kids beyond raising them to be economically responsible. Just as you and your partner need to come to common ground on the emotions accompanying money, so will your children have their feelings, that they will need to learn to navigate regarding money. While there is more to add to the emotional side of things, it all starts with getting it in writing and setting clear expectations through the spending agreement.

# | 13 |

# Investing in Emotional
# Capital

G rowing up is an emotional challenge for any child. Money
introduces a new layer of complexity. If kids don't have to
work for money, they might struggle with a sense of direction
in life. They can become dependent and "fail to launch," as was
explored in the previous chapter. They might miss out on the satisfaction of hard work and dedication to a financial goal. They might
worry that their friends are interested in them only because of their
money, or they might be tempted to use money to "buy" friendships.
These problems haunt kids and breed feelings of inadequacy—or,
even more problematic, feelings of superiority to others.

Erin shares, "Just the other day, my daughter came to me and
said, 'Those kids don't want to come to my house because of me;
they want to come to my house because of my house.' I was heartbroken. At such a young age, my daughter was wrestling with the
nature of friendship and experiencing that her material goods held
more value to some than her attributes."

It's right to recognize that kids might struggle emotionally when money comes. A landmark study from Purdue University shows that, beyond a certain healthy level, more money "tends to be associated with reduced life satisfaction and a lower level of well-being."

We all work to build financial capital to invest in all kinds of things that create value. But do you know how to build emotional capital to invest in successful relationships? Consider for a moment: What is your "emotional net worth?"

In life, you also have *emotional* assets and liabilities. Your emotional assets create happiness—emotional capital—for yourself and those who are important to you. This emotional capital includes the levels of "pride, delight, tranquility, passion, commitment, care, and trust"—and love—people have for you and that you have for yourself. By contrast, emotional liabilities create "anger, hatred, anxiety, and stress" in yourself and others. They deplete your emotional bank account.

Ironically, many high-net-worth families suffer from negative emotional capital. Knowing that your emotional capital is at risk when resources come is a significant first step in fighting against common trends.

Specifically, children are at risk from the lack of emotional capital their parents demonstrate. Parenting expert and psychologist Steve Biddulph writes that "rich kids are neglected. It's an odd combination of high expectations but a low emotional connection. Expensive private schools I consult tell me this all the time—the job of parenthood has been abrogated to others." In his practice, Biddulph sees many kids in after-school care until 9 p.m. or packed off to board at schools only blocks from their homes. "These parents don't raise their children; they just manage them." Children in this situation often have difficulty adjusting to adulthood because of emotional abandonment.

Additionally, wealth creators tend to be pressed for time. As a result, they overlook some significant issues in a teen's life. They're likely to be hyper-critical and, at the same time, paradoxically, give their children too much independence.

"The disturbing fact is that, [especially] among teens, closeness to parents is inversely correlated to affluence," says Dr. Cheryl Rampage, clinical psychologist at Northwestern University. Affluent parents are more likely to be elsewhere than at home. "Affluent teens may also feel that they don't matter in their families' lives if they are never asked to contribute economically if they have few household chores, and if they are not needed."

One kid shared his experience: "I went to a good private school, got music lessons, got any sports equipment I needed, etc. But the emotional side of things was such a dumpster fire that I grew up terrified of everyone and unable to connect to others healthily. Poverty is no joke, but neither is growing up emotionally starved."

Another child shares her perspective, "I also grew up quite wealthy but with neglectful parents who just never were there emotionally. As a child, I got a lot of material stuff, like games and movies, but they never wanted to spend time with me or my siblings." This time deprivation is common. Parents who can afford to distract their children with material things often get caught up in the trap of not spending meaningful time with them.

So, how can you help your kids navigate the emotional side of money and end up contributing to society? We've compiled a list of strategies I discovered in my interviews to help you raise emotionally resilient kids and protect your relationship with them.

## Strategy #1 – Spend Time with Them

Biddulph says the way to build emotional capital with your family is to prioritize experiences and time spent with your children. He pleads, "To do something: change your working hours or even take a year off to drive around the country. This works even when kids are in high school—I get letters all the time from people. They never regret it. 'We got to know our kids again,' they tell me."

The experts agree: buy experiences rather than things for your family. Researchers know people are "happier when they spend their money on experiential purchases rather than material ones." And I saw this in the stories I've collected as well. The happiest people were those who prioritized meaningful experiences with their loved ones. So, invest in experiences with your children to nurture their happiness and fulfillment and build up your own emotional capital. Shared experiences create memories that hold sentimental value and make emotional connection and closeness.

Jed, a successful entrepreneur, says, "Things that depreciate never create happiness, but experiences appreciate over time. It's the notion of compound emotional interest." He takes the family on an annual international adventure. They've visited places like Japan, Morocco, Peru, Nepal, and Singapore. In Nepal, they worked together on a service project that he says was "far more impactful than playing on the beaches in Thailand would've been." On a trip to India with his family, they traveled in third-class trains and explored the impoverished towns. His goal was to teach his children, through direct exposure, that there are several different ways to live. These trips aren't easy to schedule, so he says, "You have to be willing to pick up and leave!"

They don't have to be extravagant experiences to build up emotional capital, either. Simple time dedicated to your children is the best antidote to emotional deprivation and an excellent way to build emotional capital on both sides. Time spent reading with them, worshiping, traveling, playing games, or working with them —these are experiences they will treasure more than the stuff you give them. Find those blocks of time with your kids and keep them sacred.

## Strategy #2 – Say "No" A lot

While it's natural to want to do anything and everything to support our children, avoid fulfilling their every request. The word "no" helps them develop realistic expectations in life. It's important to teach children to *want* and not to *get* sometimes. "Children learn to be grateful when they don't get everything they ask for."

Erica, a skilled doctor, tells her children, "I love you and will always love you. But I am the parent. That means sometimes you won't get what you want because it isn't best for you." We owe our children tough love, she says. That doesn't mean being mean—it means putting much effort into setting and enforcing rules consistently. It means setting boundaries. Another interviewee applies this when his kids have a big decision to make. Often, they turn to him for advice. He responds, "I love you. I'll listen to you but won't decide for you." This teaches his children from a young age how to think for themselves.

## Strategy #3 – Require Children to Work

Children can only learn specific life lessons with real work, like self-discipline and a sense of accomplishment. A friend of mine says, "You can only take pride in what you earn," not what you get for nothing. "They cannot circumvent the grind if they're going to be successful in life." Handing out too much money in return for no effort stalls the development of pride in accomplishment. Another interview said, "By giving things to my children, I rob them of the pride of doing it on their own." Whether that's as simple as making their bed or making their way in the world, do you want to rob your kids of that opportunity for growth?

In Michelle Obama's book *Becoming,* she discusses this—though they had an entire staff to clean and take care of daily tasks, she required her kids to do chores while living at the White House. She emphasized teaching them responsibility and instilling a sense of normalcy despite their unique circumstances. Doing chores was part of their routine to ensure they remained grounded and learned valuable life skills.

Service helps the children of excess, specifically, but all children and people generally find meaning in life. Help small children donate used clothes or toys. Involve them in service projects. Challenge them to do kind things for each other. As they age, find opportunities to make a difference in your local community through service projects, food banks, and volunteering opportunities. Each little act of kindness serves as something good to put out in the world and a teaching moment for your children.

## Strategy #4 – Set a Good Example

While these are all strategies to help strengthen your children's resilience to emotional difficulties, the best approach is demonstrating resilience. If you want your children to be selfless, exemplify selflessness as parents who restrain your use of your resources. Show your children that you find pride and satisfaction in accomplishments rather than acquisitions. One interviewee said, "If you are driven, self-reliant, and have high self-esteem, your kids will likely be the same. But if you have been financially enabled, are codependent, and have low self-esteem, then your kids are more likely to be the same." This is true for any core attribute. If you want to instill a sense of anything in your children, an efficient way to move the needle is to model that behavior yourself. Above all, model gratitude yourself: talk about how grateful you are for them, the prosperity you enjoy, and the love of others in your life.

## Strategy #5 – Love Them

The best way to build up emotional capital is to stay close to those you love. Ask them for their opinions and then listen, particularly about their friends, their feelings, and critical issues like alcohol and drug use. Avoid lectures. Just listen. This way, you can make them comfortable discussing essential things without fear. By being a human to your children, you can relate and form a relationship that helps increase emotional capital for both parties. As you continuously show that you love and prioritize your kids over your material possessions, they will learn their value and feel your love for them.

By saying no and teaching them hard work, you will be able to build up some resiliency against some of the money's greatest pitfalls, like entitlement or feelings of superiority. Setting a good example for them gives them behavior to model that will set them up for success. When it comes to your kids, there are few things as important as investing in emotional capital.

# | 14 |

# The Speed Bumps of Change

Like your Circle A relationship(s), prosperity can deeply affect your Circle B relationships or those with your close family and friends. Money can have a positive impact on relationships, amplifying them for good. But it also comes with some speed bumps you might not anticipate. Friends and extended family will also be affected by changes in your life and the decisions you make regarding money, and you'll want to have a clear framework for navigating whatever surfaces.

New friends may come into the picture—people who weren't with you when you were at a lower point on Money Mountain suddenly emerge now that you are at the peak. This may cause you to become wary of people's intentions when pursuing a friendship with you or your close loved ones.

Old friends may suddenly look to you to invest or to give to causes that are important in their lives. You may be unsure of when and how to navigate these inbound requests. It may be difficult to travel or participate in activities with friends. Who is expected to foot the bill? Are feelings or pride going to get hurt if you decide to pay or not? Will friends feel pressured to upgrade their experiences to match whatever you are doing? Though you won't want it to, or you may be surprised when it does, money will impact your relationship with your kids.

These are just a few examples of how relationships may change when intersecting them with money. Often unintentionally and even unwillingly, relationship dynamics can change when disparity arises in the climb of Money Mountain. When a relationship is close, the effects are even more painful.

## A Chasm Between Friends

His entire life, Taylor and his best friend Casey were inseparable. In their adult years, they lived minutes apart, and they shared everything. They compared notes on how to raise kids, the highs and lows of climbing Money Mountain, and the trials of life. When, rather suddenly, Taylor found himself at the peak. At the same time, his best friend was experiencing a failing company that put his family in a stressful financial bind. Rather than climbing in tandem, the two friends found themselves on opposite ends of the mountain with a chasm between them.

Taylor was having a hard time adjusting to life at the peak. He had very real problems like, 'How do I raise my kids without spoiling them? How is it fair that I have so much while those I love are struggling?" Casey, likewise was experiencing very real problems like, "How do we turn this around?" They each desperately wanted to do as they had always done by sharing everything and talking through these pains as they were experiencing them, but they felt like they couldn't. They were at two entirely different places on the mountain.

While there was no jealousy or tension, and there were no ill feelings between the two friends, there was still a distance that left each friend extremely lonely. They used to be able to share *every-thing*, and now the biggest thing on both of their minds was off limits— they simply couldn't discuss things in the way they used to, and it created a divide. Taylor felt isolated from everyone that he felt closest to and ultimately kept his difficulties to himself.

He isn't alone in this sentiment. While some may assume that wealth creators have no problems and become aggravated by big disparities in income, the pressures and problems of having money are real. A loose but well-quoted proverb states, "He who has nothing is free to wish for a thousand things, while he who has everything wishes for only one thing." That "thing" often being meaningful relationships.

When you have resources, a new, and oftentimes uncomfortable, phenomenon occurs. Just as your kids start to see you as a bank, others in your life may naturally gravitate to you when they need money. Your sister wants a loan to buy private training for her daughter, the sports prodigy. A friend needs cash to start a multi-level marketing business. Your cousin says he can't cover the payments on your ailing aunt's home care and asks if you would lend him some money to tide him over. Your best friend comes and asks to borrow money to save his business. If faced with any of these situations, what would you actually say?

I couldn't find a playbook for how to lend money when a family member or a good friend asks for a loan. Most people just figure it out on their own through trial and error, which can lead to some painful experiences.

A lot of emotional questions come into play: What if they don't pay you back? Will it get awkward? Will you still be friends?

The negative impact this dynamic can have on a life is huge. Here are a few strategies that others have implemented to navigate loaning money to family and friends.

### Example #1 – Anonymous Giving

Issac stresses out whenever he goes to family events. He knows something will be going on in someone's life—sickness, unemployment, need for a loan—and all the eyes will turn to him. There is an expectation that he will solve whatever problem arises. He genuinely wants to help in any way he can, and over the years, he's done a lot for this family, but it often goes unappreciated.

He paid for a family cabin just to find himself owning all the responsibility for it—keeping it up in summer and making sure things don't break down in the winter. He personally doesn't want the cabin but can't sell it for fear of hurting the family. Despite his generosity, he gets asked all the time for more and more money. One day, a relative even asked him if he would buy them a vacation home in a resort area, using guilt techniques to push their agenda. These scenarios put such a strain on his family dynamics that they took the joy out of giving. Now, when he is approached, he answers with a strong "no." He uses his financial team as the excuse, saying he'll take it up with them. But, still wanting to contribute to his family whom he loves, he continues to donate anonymously for certain family priorities, like upkeep for a disabled niece. Anonymous giving and learning how to say no are how he solved being perceived as the family bank.

## Example #2 – Draw a Line in the Sand

A high net-worth individual, Owen, had a brother-in-law who was a good guy but had a lot of minor money troubles that seemed to stack up—he lost a job, needed a month's rent, and had a side project going ("that might pay off"). Each time he asked for help, Owen obliged. It went on and on, just small amounts, always with an excuse attached, "'Til I get a paycheck," and so forth. Over time, however, the requests grew. "I want to do a remodel." He asked, "Please buy this house for me so I can flip it." Then one day, he asked for a staggering few million so he could quit his job and start a business. Owen looked over the business plan; it was a lazy plan that probably wouldn't work. At that point, Owen's wife, fed up with the "guilting," wrote an email to the whole family: "Can we please just be family? We're sick of being The Bank."

Owen decided enough was enough and told his brother-in-law, "Look, we love you, we've tried hard to help you in the past, but in the future, we're going to try and support you in other ways. Here's a decent sum of money but a fraction of what you asked for, and that's the end of it." The brother-in-law took offense and wouldn't talk to him for a while. But then he went out and got a job, and now he makes a good living for his family. His self-esteem has changed. He's happy and no longer trying to ride the coattails of his family. It was a little awkward at first, but drawing a positive line in the sand paid off in social-emotional benefits for everyone involved.

### Example #3 – Give More, Once

One financial guru discovered an interesting strategy when loaning to friends and family. Michelle's brother came to her and asked for $50,000 "to get on his feet with his business." Well, it turns out that another sibling had already given him a lot of money, but the situation with his business hadn't changed. So, Michelle gave him $10,000 more than he asked for and said, "This is it; this is all that I'm prepared to give you, so don't ask again." That way, she could still help out her sibling but also prevent him from coming to the well over and over.

These experiences illustrate how money can hurt your relationships with your friends and family, but they also provide strategies for navigating these situations in ways that can work well for you. The likelihood of a personal loan going wrong is pretty high. According to one study, "Among those who have lent money . . . with the expectation of being paid back, the survey found that 59 percent had something bad happen. Forty-two percent of the lenders were not repaid, so they lost money, and 26 percent experienced a damaged relationship with the borrower."

Shannon, a successful entrepreneur shares: "Most of the money I've loaned to people has never come back to me. So, now I've officially quit lending money. Friendships have gotten painful. We've suffered so much stress from the time and energy trying to collect it, and then just to lose it—well, it's more than annoying. It's emotionally hard."

Of course, there are exceptions. One man tells this story:

*I helped a guy out some fifteen years ago. He called me crying. His parents had been caring for his mentally disabled sister, but they were dying. He explained he couldn't afford to live and pay for his sister's full-time care. So I lent him $50,000. I liked him, and I liked that he was doing it for his sister. I knew him well, and I trusted him to do right. I thought, if I never got the money back on that one, I'd have been just fine. Then three years ago, I got a check in the mail just out of the blue. It was for the whole amount. That does happen, but it's rare—very rare.*

## To Loan, or Not to Loan

So, how do you decide when to loan and when not to? A good rule of thumb is to anticipate not receiving a return on your investment and only to loan money if it's money you can "afford to lose." Here's a "Red, Yellow, Green" formula for deciding what you can "afford to lose":

- **Red:** If they're asking for a huge amount of money, you should act on the contracting guidelines (I outline some below). Make sure you evaluate the request thoroughly with your team of advisors and then think it through.
- **Yellow:** The money they're asking for is important to you, and you don't want to lose it. But if you did, it wouldn't be the end of the world.
- **Green:** Hand it out and stop worrying about it. It won't affect you, but it will benefit them.

Of course, you can always make a gift of the money. Remember to make a clear distinction between a gift and a loan. When you make it a gift, make it simple. Just give it to them and make it clear that you do *not* expect to be paid back.

When you *do* decide to make a loan to friends or family:

**Ask yourself, "Is this an asset problem or a behavior problem?"** Ultimately, you can't throw money (an asset) at a behavior problem and expect a good outcome. If you've given money before, or they have gone to others for support, and their behavior hasn't changed, it is very likely that pointing more money at the problem won't solve it. Instead, the behavior needs to change before more money will be effective. A single mother who's working to pay the bills but her car (asset) is broken down has an asset problem. To solve it, you need an asset (car or money). But if your kid keeps saying they'll make better choices (behavior) but they need help financially (assets) to get back on track, that's a behavior problem, and throwing assets at it won't change their behavior.

**Get it in writing.** Make a contract and both of you sign it. The contract should include the date of the loan, the amount of the loan, the minimum payments and the period (monthly, yearly, etc.), the interest rate (if applicable), the due date for payment in full, and the consequences of defaulting on the loan. You might think, "How can I subject my sister or my old college friend to something as impersonal as a contract?" A contract can avoid miscommunication and limit hard feelings later on. Consider including provisions requiring advance notice of missed deadlines or other requested changes. A structured contract allows both parties to walk away from the engagement successfully preserving the relationship.

**Prepare to lose your money.** Such a loss could permanently damage your relationship with the borrower. You should decide upfront how you will respond in your heart and mind if they default. By committing to not lend money to friends and family you don't want to lose and expect to not get paid back, you can avoid straining your closest relationships.

For people who are really in need but you'd rather not become a lender, there are other ways to help. You can review business plans and budgets and give the benefit of your knowledge and expertise. You can help them identify lenders, investors, or connections. Or, if they can work for you in some way, they can earn the money. I, of course, would love everyone to be able to give as much as they feel they are able. But, like most things in life, clear boundaries and ground rules for giving are important in creating a broader impact.

Regardless, the decision to loan or not to loan is a deeply personal one, with a lot of emotional implications. Take the time to determine what strategy works best for you and your family in advance and then hold to that boundary you set with your loved ones. This can help you protect your relationships and your assets.

## Enlist Help

Remember that you enlist a team to help you manage the logistics of money, so it only makes sense to have a team to help you and your family navigate the emotions of money. Just as your logistical team (investor, lawyer, accountant, etc.) meets and gives you advice on your investments, so can your emotional team act as a tool to help you navigate the social and emotional complexities that come with money.

One entrepreneur says, "I have my own personal board of directors. It's not a company. It's not an institution. It's just a group of people I depend on for counsel and wisdom in all areas of my life."

Some of his "directors" are finance professionals he trusts to give him sound guidance on his money, but not all. This man's board of directors includes his wife, his dad, a former business partner, a college professor who deeply influenced him, a personal trainer, a beloved religious leader, and a coach he had in high school. In other words, it's a diverse group with assorted viewpoints who will give him what he calls "360-degree advice"—counsel from a lot of different perspectives. He intentionally avoids including only "yes men" in this council; he has gone out of his way to recruit "directors" who will challenge him. As he wrestles with different things that come up in life, he goes to his board of directors often.

Sometimes they all meet with him together over lunch. Usually, he counsels with each director separately. "I don't trust it when people all tell me the same things. If they had different opinions, it would be much better. I need to listen to the differences."

He uses his board to guide his planning, advise him on difficult problems, and just brainstorm creatively about things on his mind.

One particularly effective use of his board is to account to them for progress on his goals. He shows them where he is with his goals —where he should be or wants to be—and then he asks what he might do to break through obstacles or find a better path to the goal. "I'm always surprised when the best ideas come from people you wouldn't expect. A high school coach just sees the world differently from a conservative money manager. That's why I listen to everybody." Without his board, he says he would be seriously disabled in making tough decisions. "No one person has all the good ideas. But when they get together, ideas build on ideas, and soon we're on to a solution nobody saw coming."

Your emotional team can help you navigate through the changed dynamics of your Circle B relationships. This doesn't account for every situation you will have with family and friends, but it hopefully gives you some helpful frameworks to center your relationships and guide you through some of the hardships that money can bring, specifically with the relationships that matter most to you—your partner, children, and friends.

Protecting strong Circle A and Circle B relationships, making sure you don't lose what's most important, are crucial steps in retooling your factory into one that produces Good.

With your inner purpose established, and your relationships protected, it's only natural to start looking outward to your Circle C relationships, or community, and consider how to have a broader impact to create a legacy that you're proud of. Which you can better do now that you are prepared for the speed bumps of change.

# LEGACY

"If you want to live, leave a legacy. Make a mark on the world that can't be erased."

**– MAYA ANGELOU**

# | 15 |

# The Ticking Time Bomb


Warren Buffett's right-hand man, Charlie Munger, was asked if "leaving his kids a bunch of money would ruin their drive and ambition."

"Of course it will," Charlie said. "But you still have to do it."

"Why?" the friend asked.

"Because if you don't give them the money, they'll hate you."

Charlie Munger is well-known for quips like this, but he's right. Because of this reality, many children of wealth creators struggle to find their level of success. They miss out on the character-building that comes from trying to make it themselves. There is less fear of failure because the parental safety net is always there. This begs the question, how will you distribute your money? What kind of mark will you leave behind once you're gone? How will you distribute the assets you've earned in life, post-death?

You may have assumed like I had, that you would leave everything to your family. Either through a shared asset or a trust, I would pass on whatever resources I had to my children and grandchildren. I even went as far as to surmise that these assets—like a cabin or vacation home, for example—would serve as the vehicle through which I could ensure that my family made positive memories together when I was no longer around.

That's why, when interviewing a man I admire who has built a strong legacy, I was shocked to hear his conclusion: "Shared assets ruin families."

As I talked to more people, I surprisingly discovered that story after story supported this assessment. I've concluded that a shared asset is not the same thing as leaving a lasting legacy, and in fact, it often has the opposite effect, with family conflict stemming from the asset in question. In extreme cases, the shared asset actually acts to destroy the intended legacy.

I pressed the man further and asked, "What do you mean shared assets ruin families?" He told me the story of a farmer in small-town America. The farmer had worked hard to acquire and maintain a large piece of land with several properties. When he died, he split the sum of the property and gave it to his two sons as a parting gift. The land was excellent and in a prime location. The father sincerely wanted to help his sons and give them something nice when he passed. He could think of nothing better than to give it to his posterity, believing there was no greater legacy to leave.

At first, this was the right assessment. His sons enjoyed the land and properties, took great care of them, and, in turn, gifted them to their children. But his well-intentioned gift was a time bomb thrown into his family tree. By the third generation, relationships between family members were completely destroyed. All members of the family split into factions. Even though it wasn't land they had earned individually, they all felt entitled to it. They all felt a deep ownership over the land. The conflict escalated to a degree where family members hated each other. Why? Because each family member was convinced that other family members received "the better land" or didn't "use it in the right way."

What started as a generous gift initiated an entitlement mentality and became the source of tremendous familial discord and estrangement. How sad would their grandpa be to discover that his generous gift to his children had caused such conflict among his grandchildren? It begs a straightforward question: Do you think he would have given the land and properties to his children if he knew what the result would be further down his family tree?

In countless interviews, I found this pattern. Houses, cabins, vacation homes, and other assets as common as grandma's jewelry or a family piano, were generously gifted to posterity, only to tear apart family dynamics and relationships for years to come. It happens on a daily basis, but it also goes back generations.

In the 1800s, a pioneer couple settled in a remote region of the Mountain West. Part of their settlement included a beautiful canyon that they owned and revered. They painstakingly worked the land and the area to make the canyon and adjacent land their home.

While they had no children, they belonged to a large family that comprised most of the town and neighboring towns. The entire family would gather for a large reunion each year, enjoying each other's company and making fond memories. They continued this tradition for over 30 years, which was the entirety of this couple's adult life in the region. The couple lived a long, fulfilling life and died within 2 months of each other with their family intact and proud of their hard work.

Once this couple passed, the family immediately began to fray and fragment. Days after their death, there was backstabbing, rewriting of wills, and even conflict escalating to shootouts. By the time the next family reunion rolled around, it was canceled and never revisited in subsequent years. What caused such a close-knit family to disintegrate so rapidly? It all came back to the canyon.

The couple had set no precedent for how the land was to be distributed once they passed. Nieces, nephews, siblings, and distant cousins determined they should receive the canyon. Each claimed that the couple had promised the land to them, and each felt a strong sense of ownership and entitlement to what they assumed was theirs. Conflict over the land grew so stifling that family members couldn't even gather together without arguments arising. The asset became the source of a family's separation and caused a tight-knit family tree to fray.

Land, property, house, and even a family business—any physical asset given freely in the name of a legacy, will, without fail, break families apart. If not in the first generation, often by the second or third generation. As this person cheekily explained to me, if there's no conflict between your kids, there are always in-laws as the new family dynamic opens up an even greater opportunity for disagreement, and if it's not the first generation, it's the second. It is literally a time bomb that will go off at some point. What was even more amazing to discover was that it didn't matter how explicit a person was in defining their wishes after passing. No matter the circumstances, shared assets acted as a time bomb thrown into each family tree.

The more individuals who feel entitled to the property, the more complexity and conflict around how it *should* be used. Take a house, for example. Even if a parent explicitly states that the house should be used equally by their three children, one sibling may need money and wish to sell, while another will use it more because they live closer, and a third may not contribute at all to the upkeep. It all leads to bickering, fighting, and complaining, which creates a sad reality that far too often shared properties can't survive through generations.

A single asset can only sustain so much consumerism. And the bigger the asset the bigger the problem. Take the house again as an example. If it's split among the three siblings, contention may brew, but it may survive. But what if each of those three siblings have three children? Now the asset needs to be split nine ways. And if they have three children, it now needs to split twenty-seven ways. It quickly becomes an inverted pyramid that is no longer sustainable.

The same phenomenon exists in a family business.

## Josh's Family Business

Josh worked his entire life at his father's company, eventually becoming CEO. He deeply loved the work he was a part of and considered it his life's mission to do right by the company and do his best to succeed. When his father passed, Josh was alarmed to discover that, although none of his siblings had previously worked at the company, they would all receive equal salaries in the family business from then on. Regardless of how much they worked, each sibling would get the same monetary compensation. When work and compensation are so intertwined, it can be hard to see siblings working harder than one another and earning the same "equal" compensation.

This zapped Josh's energy out of work. He was left wondering, well, what's the point of working so hard if I could make just as much doing nothing like my other siblings? After wrestling with the new dynamic of his sibling 'employees,' he decided he couldn't take it anymore, and he ended up leaving the company in frustration, determined to find fulfillment elsewhere. Josh's father had no intention of Josh leaving his position as CEO. His greatest desire was to see his family carry on his legacy by working for and being supported by the family business. The sad reality is that gifts through assets, even those that are well intended, never survive the way the were intended to. They end up doing more harm than good to your family members who you care about. Consider the farmer who's third generation is no longer talking to each other. How would he describe this outcome to his family tree? Assets negatively effect, and sometimes ruin, relationships. And we see it with trusts as well.

## The Problem with Trusts

If you are as dismayed by the above stories as I was, your initial reaction may be similar to my thought of "I'll just liquidate." I was confident I could be saved from the shared asset eventuality by giving my children money in a trust to use once I'm gone. This is standard practice, after all, and though it can be used as a vehicle for Good, I was discouraged to discover that lacking a larger framework for how the money should be used (and often even with a framework in place), the result is far more negative than you would expect and, like assets, to use the word destruction might not be that far fetched.

Tina had worked hard her entire life and built up a handsome fortune. She was careful not to spoil her children and divided her money equally between the three of them. Tina put this money into trusts that were activated once she passed on. Each child inherited a large lump sum to use for the rest of their lives.

Though her intentions were pure, the trust amount subsequently ruined each of her children. Unaccustomed to the sudden resources they had at their fingertips, they got caught up in vices enabled by their income. They didn't have the motivation to work or make a lasting impact on the world and ultimately struggled with significant mental and physical health issues due to the choices they had made in their lives. Each squandered their inheritance and left nothing to pass on to future generations.

Finally, by setting aside money in a trust that is only accessible once you pass, you incentivize your children to desire your death. We see this time and time again throughout history. With a constant strain on familial relationships, a great king is thwarted by his children, as his demise is his children's boon. In modern times, it looks like children are trying to take over a parent's estate later in life to "protect their parents" when they are really just looking out for themselves. Though children won't typically be so dramatic as to resort to murder, money does have a powerful allure, and the strain on relationships is very real and something I wanted to avoid when planning out my legacy.

A man I interviewed expressed his genuine concern about his kids anticipating, even expecting, assets upon his death. That mentality is super dangerous while trying to foster a close-knit relationship between parent and child. This becomes particularly precarious if they plan their lives around an expectation that may or may not be met. In our interviewee's case, he doesn't have as much as they think. He doesn't discuss what is in the trust as he fears it will incentivize his death and negatively alter his relationship with his children.

Because of this, he hasn't set clear expectations, and his children are reading into his worth, estimating it to be much larger than what is actually in the bank. They are planning their lives and their retirement around an assumed inheritance. Both parties are at a detriment.

## What You Can Pass Down

Through these interviews, I saw clearly that passing down assets is like leaving a legacy of a dead-end alleyway. It might take a few generations to get to the dead end, but there is *always* a dead end. At first, I was disheartened. If you can't leave your legacy in an asset and a trust can turn sour, what are your options?

Again, you have to find what works best for you and your family, and the good news is that there are ways to do it better.

One example is a father who, wanting to avoid the destruction outlined above, has determined to save all of his wealth in a single trust and set clear parameters for giving it all away to charitable causes after he dies. While this may be a better option, it still isn't the best, as he misses an opportunity to give alongside his children while he's alive. But it does pass down his values of service and outward living.

Some parents adopt the "die with zero" mentality. They block their children from ever benefiting from the family resources. Ambassador Shelby C. Davis, a legendary investor and founder of the philanthropic Davis Funds, told his son Chris that he "would never see a penny of it because the family didn't want to rob him of the opportunity of making it on his own." Chris jokes, "They could have robbed me *just* a little." While this may seem a little harsh, it gives your children something valuable: opportunity. They can have the ability to determine their future. Some parents add to this opportunity by only paying for things like education, down payments on houses, or money to start a business. They encourage their children to seize opportunities to determine their future, and in doing so, they also pass down values of independence and responsibility.

While you can't pass down shared assets and still preserve a positive legacy, you can pass down your story, values, and, above all, your Factory for Good.

As you look outward, you can pass down the opportunity for each member of your family tree to make their journey through life and establish their Factory for Good, essentially initiating a perpetuating ripple effect that extends for generations to come. That's why legacy is the last step in retooling your Factory for Good. It is the ultimate diffuser to the ticking time bomb.

# | 16 |

# The Ripple Effect

One summer evening, my brother Doug and I drove back to the Salt Lake Valley from a trip to St. George. The desert road was desolate and long. I decided to leverage our time together to convince my brother that he needed to grow his business—a wealth management firm started by our father. I am a natural builder and am very entrepreneurial at heart, so I was having a hard time understanding why I couldn't convince him to grow. Coming from my world of tech, I tried everything I could to convince him of the business benefits of growth, encouraging him to focus on increased funds as an incentive. He wouldn't budge. I couldn't understand why; the answer seemed so obvious.

As we talked, however, we slowly became aligned and eventually reached a clear moment of unlocking between our two perspectives. As he explained his reason for going into business and how it wasn't to make money but to protect families, I realized that his job as a wealth advisor put him in a unique position to protect family trees. He wasn't just looking after someone's assets but how they managed those assets in a way that protected the emotional strength of a family for generations to come. My brother wasn't motivated by money, but by the people he could help! There are hundreds of people who stem from a single individual. How well my brother does his job will affect hundreds of people's lives. For him, it's not about earning money to earn money.

As I explained how growth and wealth amplify every intention, my brother began to realize that even if money wasn't his focus, it could increase his opportunity to do good and make a difference in his clients' lives.

I walked away from that conversation convinced that hundreds of individuals could benefit from giving one person the opportunity to build and maintain something of value. Though I understood that prosperity is in fact finite, with the right frameworks in place, it can create a positive impact for years to come.

He walked away from that conversation, encouraged to grow his business, not for the money, but for the opportunity to be a positive influence in his clients' families for years to come.

It's a ripple effect. Each life acts as a stone thrown into time and space. There will be ripples that spread and become pervasive. Each person must decide for themselves if those ripples will have a positive or negative influence, and they also have some control over how significant an impact their life has or how sustaining their ripples are.

We both felt inspired to build as big as we could! The bigger we built, the bigger the stone we could drop in the proverbial waters of life, and the bigger the ripples of impact to those around us. This was the origin of the concept of a Factory for Good. At that moment, I realized that the more our factories output money, the more family trees we could affect and the more change we could actualize.

I knew I wanted future generations to have a foundation of opportunity in a free and safe part of the world where they have the chance to thrive and go beyond what I could achieve. If I feed you directly, I understand that you'll be hungry within a few hours. But if I can give you a skill or broader education—in short, a clear opportunity—then you can change not only your fortune but the fortune of your family tree for generations to come. This ability to positively affect a family tree is the root of the legacy I want to leave and is the root of the purpose of a Factory for Good.

Each person represents the start of a family tree, with posterity branching off their lives. If I keep my family tree healthy and thriving, my legacy doesn't stop at me but continues growing from generation to generation. This can be applied to a larger community as well. If I can look at an orchard of family trees in which the vast majority are dying, and I can pick even one to pluck and prune and make healthy and productive, then all the branches and subsequent trees from that original graft will also be healthy.

Your legacy is the long-lasting impact that you will have on future generations, your community, and the world at large. As Lin Manuel Miranda wrote, "A legacy is planting seeds in a garden you never get to see."

The stronger the legacy, the larger and longer lasting the impact in the lives of people you have not met and the greater the ripple effect on others' lives.

I am inspired to write this book and do good in the world because of the strong legacy my great-grandfather left. I've made choices in my life because of what he believed, and that, to me, is the power of a legacy. It drives my desire to create a lasting sustainable change— to positively affect as many family trees as possible. The Factory for Good is the vehicle to do just that.

Many assume that a legacy is focused solely on altruistic motives. And it's true, a legacy does cause you to look outward. The great secret, so common it has become a cliche, is that in serving others, you serve yourself. By focusing outward, you're able to strengthen your inner purpose and your relationships with others. You create a personal legacy that lives after you pass and improves your life as you live.

This realization can be a powerful motivator in anyone's life, especially those who are actively searching for a higher purpose.

A young man in his twenties who got rich on Wall Street thought he couldn't be happier.

"I felt so important," he says. "At twenty-five, I could go into any restaurant in Manhattan just by picking up the phone. I could be in the second row at the Knicks-Lakers game just by hinting. Because of how successful I was, it was someone else's job to make me happy."

He took full advantage of his situation and used his money primarily in indulgence. Unfortunately, drugs and alcohol soon dominated his life. He got entirely caught up in the vices that his newfound financial freedom enabled.

While on vacation, he picked up *The History of the Civil Rights Movement* and started to read. The image of the Freedom Riders stepping off their bus into an infuriated mob seared itself into his mind. "I told myself that if I'd been alive in the '60s, I would have been on that bus. But I was lying to myself. There were plenty of injustices out there—rampant poverty, swelling prison populations, a sexual assault epidemic –" to name a few.

He realized that chasing surface-level happiness with his money was not helping to fix any problems in the world. He also realized that by focusing on money, he had lost the ability to be truly happy. That day, he decided to shift his attention and fundamentally change his life.

He worked his way off his addictions. He got married. He spoke in jails and juvenile detention centers about getting sober. He taught classes for kids in the foster system. He started a non-profit to help low-income families struggling with hunger. In short, he found a new purpose and began to "earn his sleep" again. "I am much happier."

He says, "I feel as if I'm making a real contribution." He had successfully found a purpose far greater than merely enjoying his financial freedom. Instead, he leveraged his financial gain to do good in the world. To use our factory analogy, he found a way to use money to amplify his happiness, retool his factory, and output Good.

This young man learned what it meant to live a meaningful life.

His journey shows how exciting it can be to look outward and consider influencing others' lives for the better. Still, several avenues can be taken to determine how much, where, and how to give. It can be overwhelming to try and navigate everything related to the world of philanthropic giving and how to build a legacy, so much so that it can be challenging to begin giving or recognize the impact your efforts have on the world.

Establishing a simple framework that works for you is a great place to start when seeking to create a lasting legacy.

## Strategy #1 – Life in Thirds

Andrew Carnegie is a man whose lasting legacy is well-known. Born in a one-room weaver's cottage in Scotland, Carnegie emigrated to America as a youth and got a job as a telegraph operator in Pittsburgh. There, he benefited from the generosity of a successful local businessman, Colonel James Anderson, who opened his library of 400 books to any working boys. Unable to go to school, Carnegie avidly took advantage of Anderson's library and dutifully and thoroughly educated himself on all things business, history, and beyond. He said, "I resolved, if ever wealth came to me, that other poor boys might receive opportunities similar to mine." He wrote out a simple framework for his life: spend the first third of my life getting all the education I can, spend the next third making all the money I can, and spend the last third giving it all away for worthwhile causes.

True to his word, he spent the first third of his life studying and working to learn. Then, he worked to earn and eventually became one of the wealthiest steel manufacturers of his day. He could have continued creating, but he quit his businesses in his sixties to become a full-time philanthropist. He stuck to his framework and focused on giving all his money to worthwhile causes. As one of his many charitable endeavors, he paid homage to the generosity he experienced as a young working boy and funded more than 3,000 libraries across the USA and a college for the children of working-class Americans. Now known as Carnegie-Mellon University, it is one of the premier research universities in the world. Long after Carnegie's death, his legacy continues to benefit the lives of millions of people.

**Strategy #2 – The 40-30-30 Rule**

After making money in the tech sector, Lee navigated the prosperity paradox intentionally and built a Factory for Good. He established a mantra of "40-30-30," where he dedicated 40% of his wealth to charity, 30% to his future, and 30% to enjoying life.

By placing the majority of his resources in a position to look outward, Lee made an incredible impact in various philanthropic avenues. This dedication to leveraging his money to amplify its impact was made even more apparent in his establishment of two non-profits. Both programs were designed to break the cycle of poverty by providing individuals with the means to obtain education and vocational training, thereby empowering them to secure better employment opportunities and improve their quality of life.

Under Lee's guidance, the non-profits gained momentum and expanded their reach, impacting the lives of thousands of individuals and families around the world. His dedication to the program's mission and his commitment to humanitarian service helped establish a flagship initiative to alleviate poverty and promote self-reliance through education. This left a lasting impact on countless individuals and communities worldwide. Likewise, his non-profit has significantly contributed to international development by pioneering innovative approaches to poverty alleviation and fostering partnerships that enable positive social and economic change.

## Strategy #3 – $5,000 Miracles

You don't need to have a lot or give a lot to make an incredible impact. One of my favorite interviews describes a philosophy of "$5,000" miracles. That check size could often mean paying a month's rent, providing much-needed child care, or getting a car for a single mom who needs it to survive. One person I worked closely with exemplified this philosophy before he had money to give. He often gathered people together to chip in small amounts of money to help individuals he encountered.

Once, he gathered the support of nearly fifty people to chip in and buy a car for a single mom whose car broke down. His group texts advertising a good cause and asking for whatever amount people felt like they could donate at the time always made my day. He knew how to make an impact and build a lasting legacy long before he came close to summiting Money Mountain.

Each example demonstrates an intentional approach to building a vehicle with a lasting impact—a legacy each individual could be proud of. It's important to note that worthwhile causes are not just giving to charity. You may find deep meaning and opportunities to look outward through various avenues. They can be religious, community, service, or cultivating family relationships. Even a for-profit organization can do a lot in the world that is altruistic. The important thing is finding a worthwhile cause that works for you and how you want to leave your legacy.

That is what a legacy embodies: a way of tying your prosperity, your family, and your community together in a positive, lasting way. We all feel this responsibility to do some form of good. This is your opportunity to leave your imprint on the world, but more importantly, it's the formula for lasting happiness, a feeling no amount of money can't buy. By looking outward and developing a simple framework you can easily follow, you're on your way to establishing a legacy and building your Factory for Good, and ultimately extending a positive ripple effect.

# | 17 |

# What Good Looks Like

I have talked about a Factory for Good from a theoretical standpoint—that as you carefully retool your factory to use money as an amplifier and closely follow the three pillars of purpose, relationships, and legacy, you can produce Good. I fundamentally believe that this Factory for Good is the key to living a full and happy life.

This is a great definition from a conceptual perspective. But there is a more tactile definition that involves the actual vehicle for creating a lasting, sustainable legacy in your life. It gives you the focus and guidance to act on and measure your impact.

A Factory for Good is typically personal, created from gaining your own experience, and disciplined in reporting and execution. But what does Good look like? How can you spot it in the wild or work to make your efforts into a Factory for Good?

At the heart of every Factory for Good lies a foundational commitment to core values that transcend traditional business metrics. Here, success is measured not by quarterly earnings but by the well-being it fosters among communities, the opportunities it creates, and the footprints it leaves behind.

## Taikichiro Mori

Taikichiro Mori is a great example of choosing a cause that was personal to him. When he was eighteen, the Great Kantō Earthquake hit his hometown of Tokyo. A 33-foot tsunami roared through the city, drowning thousands of people, followed by a massive firestorm called a "dragon twist." Forty-five thousand people died in this tornado of fire in Tokyo's center. Fortunately, Mori survived, but he never forgot the terror of that day.

After a prosperous career as dean of the Yokohama University business school, he retired at 55. Not feeling ready to quit work, he took over his father's modest real-estate firm and was soon possessed by a new mission. Remembering the severe suffering in the wake of the Kantō Earthquake, Mori began to study how to build structures that would withstand earthquakes. He chose a Factory for Good personal to his pain as a younger man. He translated this pain into a clear intention: build "smart buildings" with their foundations resting on a complex system of rollers that keep the buildings stable while the ground moves under them. In addition to installing spring-like shock absorbers to soak up the energy of the pitching earth, this became his life's focus. While his approach was technical, he intended to prevent catastrophic damage in the case of an earthquake.

Armed with this clear intention, his progress was measurable in the number of buildings he could enhance with life-saving technology. At its height, the Mori Company owned more than eighty buildings in the downtown section of the capital city.

It's important to note that a Factory for Good doesn't mean giving away or absolving yourself entirely from money. In fact, by 1991, Forbes ranked Mori as the wealthiest man in the world. The key is the lasting impact that an intentional, personal, and experienced Factory for Good has on the world. Far more critical to Mori than his fortune was his incredible legacy of buildings that can hold out against violent earthquakes, thus saving countless lives. By addressing a problem, Mori successfully established a lasting legacy and created immense value for the world. In short, he produced Good.

## The Stewart Family

Ellie works as a college counselor at her local high school. She works with juniors and seniors applying for college and scholarships. Because she works so closely with these students, she has a unique view of their financial situations and witnesses many kids discouraged by the impending costs of steep student loans.

As a couple, Ellie and Mike decided that this was where they'd focus all of their giving. They chose a cause that was personal to what Ellie saw daily. After exploring several different avenues of how they wanted to make a difference, they created an anonymous scholarship which enables all of Ellie's students who are in need to afford college. Every student in that school who wants to attend college will do so through their scholarship fund. It's extra fun for them because Ellie works so closely with the students utilizing their scholarship to achieve their academic goals. The Stewarts have found a way to give back to their community simply but effectively.

The couple only supports students who are looking for an opportunity, are willing to work hard, and want to improve themselves. By being able to closely monitor this and the output of the scholarships given, they are more motivated to provide and be engaged in their local community. Ellie and Mike share this experience, and they're beginning to engage their children as well, hoping to have this be their lasting legacy.

## What Good Entails

While every factory will look different and have its own unique branding and flavor, there are a few things that are consistent across the board. We've gone ahead and created a template (see Appendix) that each Factory for Good should be able to fit into. As I work to determine to which causes I should contribute, I run an organization's information through this template and use it to compare one factory to another.

A Factory for Good should be able to succinctly prove that they are legitimate and that they measure and report on performance. They should also be able to answer who they are, whom they help, why they are different from other organizations, and if they have a local, international, or national impact. Furthermore, suppose you are either creating your Factory for Good or assessing one to which you would like to donate. In the case of assessing a 'factory' to which you'd like to donate, there should be a series of donation options, either time or money, through which you can chart a clear impact score to compare and visualize the impact of your donation or resource spend, and there should be a clear tie to one of your core values.

The most robust factories are built for a clear and meaningful purpose. This purpose acts as the North Star, guiding every decision and initiative. It's about solving real problems, meeting genuine needs, and making the world slightly better with every product or service offered.

No factory can thrive in isolation. A Factory for Good nurtures solid and healthy relationships within its walls and the broader community. These relationships are built on trust, respect, and mutual benefit.

Unlike traditional factories focused on short-term outputs, a Factory for Good is deeply invested in the long-term impacts of its actions. It seeks to leave a legacy that future generations will look back on with pride, demonstrating a commitment to sustainable practices and ethical excellence.

Finally, a Factory for Good is marked by an unwavering commitment to continual improvement. It is an organization that learns from successes and failures, always striving to better fulfill its mission. It embraces feedback, encourages dialogue, and remains open to change, ensuring it can adapt and thrive in a changing world. This is, in essence, what Good looks like.

## | 18 |

# How to Build a Factory
# for Good

You've been in the business of inputting your time and effort to create value or money. Now we will switch from using money as the output to an amplifier in that process, focusing on leaving a lasting impact on the world. As you make this shift, you can successfully retool your factory to one that produces Good.

## Use Money as an Amplifier

Jeremy was always really good at making money. He worked extremely hard, and there was a direct correlation between his hard work and the success of his business. When his first factory reached a level of output that covered his basic needs, he was determined to continue working and make even more.

In my interview, I asked him: "Why are you still working?" I was convinced he continued climbing Money Mountain and was motivated by greed or apathy. His answer surprised me:

"I know what I'm good at—it's making money. But now I've found a reason to keep making money." He explained: "The more [money] I make, the more troubled teens I can help support."

He then explained to me that, after experiencing the power of a rehab center to help their child work through some life-altering trials, he and his wife put all of their excess funds into building rehab centers to support troubled teens. A savvy businessman, he was mainly influenced to target troubled teens in his Factory for Good because he figured that was the highest ROI he could experience. This time, instead of measuring ROI in money, he measured it in impact or his ability to fundamentally change someone's life.

It was a lightbulb moment for me. A Factory for Good doesn't necessarily mean stopping the production of money. Instead, money becomes a vital amplifier of a lasting impact that creates an element of good in the world.

On the surface, Jeremy chose to continue climbing Money Mountain. However, it wasn't because he wanted to make money to have more money or more things. He continued climbing Money Mountain because he had found a Factory for Good that he was deeply passionate about, and he wanted more money to act as an even greater amplifier of this cause. He instinctively knew that if he could make more money and invest it into this Factory for Good; he could have an even more significant and long-lasting impact. So, he keeps working and earning money. The more money he earns, the more he can invest in rehab centers.

Jeremy and his wife helped hundreds of kids each year to get therapy and get back on the right track. Jeremy carefully monitors where his money is going and who it will impact, and he ensures that it will continue to grow through his posterity after he is gone. In doing so, he tracks his impact on the teens that his funds help support. He maintains close relationships with them and enjoys seeing them succeed as they progress. He has even involved his kids in the effort, and it's something they can talk about and track their family values through. By translating the money he earns into a clear input toward a cause for good, he has created a lasting impact that is sustained and enduring.

This is the power of a Factory for Good. It's how to build a lasting legacy that matters to you, and it helps your family contribute to something larger than themselves; the impact is measurable and contributions are sustainable.

## Start with a Guiding Mission

To start, decide what mission will drive your efforts. Understanding what brings you joy is the first step. The next is to crystallize this joy into a mission that directs your life's work. A mission isn't just a statement; it's a compass that guides you through life's choices —where to invest your energy, time, and resources. Rooted in what brings you fulfillment, it should reflect what brings you enduring happiness and provide a clear framework for your decisions.

An excellent place to start is by analyzing your Happiness Audit. As you look over the results of your Happiness Audit, consider:

*What does it tell you about what you should live for?*

*What did you value most?*

*What brings you the most joy?*

*What is worth spending your resources on?*

Find some quiet place and probe your heart and mind to find the answers to these questions.

Then, start writing a personal mission statement—a clear and concise summary of the Purpose of Your Factory for Good. This statement is a powerful tool that clearly defines what you live for. It helps you focus on your pathway to the future, choose the goals that matter to you, and bypass the "fatal distractions" that can keep you from achieving your great purpose.

A mission statement should be succinct, memorable, and actionable—something you can refer to daily and use to align your actions. In determining your Factory's mission, explicit guiding attributes make it a powerful vehicle for lasting impact. Joseph Grenny, author of *Crucial Conversations* and a co-builder of the non-profit UNITUS, gives these principles for giving with direction and purpose:

1. Make it Personal
2. Gain Your Own Experience
3. Have Discipline

You can build a meaningful, powerful Factory for Good as you carefully do these three things. In my interviews, I found several examples of people living by these principles in their giving efforts. For those who made it personal, it became more meaningful and significantly more impactful to them and their family.

## Make it Personal

I discovered that people genuinely want to build a Factory for Good but need help figuring out where to start. The world of charitable giving and worthwhile causes can be vast and overwhelming. It can take time to pinpoint exactly where, how, and why you want to make an impact.

It helps if you make it personal. Like anything in life, you will be more motivated to participate and dedicated to a cause that resonates with you on a personal level.

Ashley, a public educator, had a son die by suicide. Heartbroken, she decided to channel her grief in efforts to help others suffering from mental illness. She volunteered each week for the suicide hotline, and raised money for mental health awareness. She found deep fulfillment by getting involved in a cause that was so personal to her.

This is deeply personal, and it may take a while to ponder and determine what matters enough to dedicate your time, energy, and money to it for the rest of your life and beyond.

We've discussed examples of what a Factory for Good is to give you a general idea of what to look for. Now that you know what the framework for a Factory for Good looks like, you only need to decide what *your* unique Factory for Good looks like. Every person is different, and where, how, and why they want to leave a lasting impact on the world will also be different. The trick is to determine what exactly is personally meaningful to you. If you have experienced mental health issues, breast cancer, or a drug-addicted child, you'll be more invested in causes dedicated to where you have personally felt the pain. It brings emotion to giving because you know the pain of not having a solution. It creates empathy for all those in the shoes that you have personally walked in.

If you were in business, you may have found product market fit by creating a solution to a defined problem that you experienced when money was the output of your factory. You can apply the same process to your Factory for Good. If you build where there is a problem to be solved, with pain that you've personally felt, you'll find a "giving/cause fit" that you'll be motivated to chase.

We may find several causes that resonate with our souls but need more time to decide which one to prioritize. The "Factory for Good Finder" is a tool that helps you navigate this process. It's a facilitator of the hard conversations to help you narrow down to your core values and where you want to make a lasting impact. It enables you to work through how you want to give and provides opportunities to explore a deeper motivation. This helps guide you to a place of intrinsic incentive to provide and helps you avoid feeling hollow.

A great way to determine where you want to make an impact is to decide what causes mean the most to you. The value wheel (see Appendix) can help guide you to your core values and what causes are attached to those values. This wheel isn't meant to be comprehensive; rather, it is a facilitator to help narrow down where you want to make an impact. By the end of this exercise, you should clearly articulate where, how, and why you want to make an impact.

Jill filled out our exercise and landed on the following giving profile:

*Figure 18-1 Example of a Giving Profile*

WHERE

# Jill's Giving Profile

Performing
Libraries
Culture

Scholarships
Arts
Institutions

Education
Acccess
Equity

Mental
Basic

Quality
Primary

Gender

Health

Trauma

**HOW**

1  National

2  International

3  National

Hands On          Hands Off

**ALIGN WITH ORGANIZATIONS THAT:**

Have a Strong Feedback Loop

Work Closely with Recipients

Focus on Donations

## Giving Target:

**Donate 100 books per month**

In the example above, Jill's core values are culture, health, and education, with specific causes for which she may be interested in donating books to her local library, fundraising for mental health institutions, or providing quality scholarships for women in marginalized neighborhoods. Here, she has a clear map of where to give. Having three giving pillars creates a mission statement, or a banner of giving, to which Jill's posterity can look. Everyone in her family knows her pillars and what she stands for.

In completing this exercise, Jill found she wanted a hands-on approach on a local scale, choosing that over international impact or simply donating funds. She had volunteered at nonprofits in the past, which allowed her to be very closely related to the recipients of her donations. She enjoyed that closeness and knew she wanted to follow a similar path in her Factory for Good. Specifically, she wanted to focus on giving one hundred books per month to local libraries. Here, she has a clear view of how to give.

Through completing our exercise, Jill saw that her lack of access to books growing up motivated her desire to give back and identified a clear strategy for starting her Factory for Good. By following the "Factory for Good Finder" below, you can likewise experience a honing in on what matters to you when you consider where, how, and why you want to give of your time and money.

## Gain Your Own Experience

Armed with a giving profile outlining where and how you want to make an impact, you still want to get a feel for what's out there before building your foundation or committing to a worthwhile cause. It's wild to me that most top donors for most charitable organizations are the founder's friends. Most people give but are interested in something other than a particular cause, such as donating because their friend asked. While giving in any form is good, having a clear guiding principle regarding where you spend your valuable resources is better.

Those I interviewed who focused on gaining their own experiences before committing to any particular cause usually did so because they still needed to be called to something. It's wise to see what's out there before committing your time, energy, and money. Dive into the middle of causes that may pique your interest! Determine which causes pull on your heartstrings when you're in the middle of doing them versus which ones aren't as impactful as you previously thought.

Justin assumed that he would immensely enjoy a hands-on approach in mentoring recipients of a scholarship fund that he took part in. He traveled to the university and spent a week as a visiting mentor, engaging in one-on-ones with dozens of students. While he recognized that this was a good thing to do, he realized in the experience that he wasn't as interested in mentoring as he previously thought. His personality and energy didn't align with mentoring in a classroom setting. He felt like he wasn't making as much of a difference with his time as he could in other places and decided to spend his resources in other worthwhile ways.

Claire experimented with several different NGOs before going on a trip to Latin America with an organization that mentored young entrepreneurs and helped them double their annual income. Seeing the direct effect a little mentoring could have in the lives of those seeking to better their lives sparked a passion in Claire's heart. This experience completely changed Claire's mindset on where she wanted to focus her attention and set her on a path to support entrepreneurial organizations with her time and money moving forward.

While you explore and interact with NGOs and nonprofits, look to develop your own opinions on an organization's strategy, how it manages its teams, and how it measures results. By experiencing both the good and bad of what exists, you will be able to develop your giving philosophy and determine what kind of organization you would like to align with going forward.

For some, this means volunteering time at as many nonprofits/worthwhile causes as possible. For others, it means researching the organizations. And for others still, it may mean making smaller donations or engaging at a smaller scale across a variety of different avenues. Whatever path you choose, several organizations fit your giving profile. To determine where you will make the most impact and what will be most impactful to you, I recommend vetting and prioritizing organizations as they come across your desk.

First, use your giving profile to determine if you should donate your time or money when an opportunity arises. Ask yourself: Does this support one of my three values? Will this help me donate nationally, internationally, or locally?

Then, consider the organization's legitimacy and the capability to trace your donation to actual impact. Cotopaxi exemplifies responsible giving, and they suggest that when considering when to give, ask yourself:

*Is it a 501c3 nonprofit or a public nonprofit?*

*Was it founded more than two years ago?*

*Does it have a website, physical address, and phone number? And have real, credible people validated this organization?*

*Have third parties validated its performance?*

*Does it have a sound and tested methodology to trace its outcomes?*

*Does 70%+ of its budget go to programs? Do they report on their impact?*

If the answer is yes to all of the above, then give your time and money willingly. If you answer no, stop and consider if this is the best use of your resources.

Other people choose to vet organizations further based on who is at the helm. They consider the capacity and character of the CEO and prefer to bet on the jockey, not the horse. This is very similar to how a VC firm would consider the leadership team of a startup before investing any significant amount of capital.

Others still consider sustainability a key indicator of whether or not to donate. Suppose there is a path to a social entrepreneurial structure and a way to ensure that your time or money isn't going into a bucket with a hole in the bottom or that people will not repeatedly return to the well. In that case, they donate more willingly than otherwise. Before donating to any cause or participating in any activity, you may ask whether this serves my broader mission statement. If it's a yes, give willingly! If it's a no, reconsider using your time, money, and efforts better.

Choose what's best for you in your decision matrix on where to donate, and know plenty of publicly available resources can help you research organizations and impact areas.

Once you've decided to donate, it's time to determine what level of impact you want to have or how much time and money you want to donate. This is best accomplished by taking the focal organization/cause and ensuring you truly understand what they do, whom you are helping, where you are helping, and how they differ from other organizations. Then it all comes down to simple math, such as how many people your donation will help.

To help me best measure the impact of my donations and ensure I stay consistent, I've come up with an impact score for each potential donation that I can use to compare one donation to another. By assigning a score to each potential donation, I can justify spending more time or money if it means an increased impact score. It also levels the playing field by making it a numbers game instead of driving decisions based purely on feeling. The impact score is made up of inputs where there are fifteen total points at stake. So if I want max impact, I'll have an impact score of fifteen, whereas a low impact might only be a three. An impact score is directly tied to the number of people you will help with your donation and how it will fundamentally change their lives, and you get bonus points if it aligns with your core values, involves your family, and if you have a gut instinct that you will have an impact. Together, these equate to a score you can use to compare and determine your level of impact. This is a key thing that can help with your larger effort to measure the impact of your giving.

## Measure the Impact

As many of the people I interviewed experienced in pursuing their first factory, they want to see a clear return on investment when they spend their time and money in their second factory. The best way to have this discipline is to measure the impact of your factory to keep yourself accountable. Many employers keep their employees responsible through KPIs or other metrics that can be measured. This helps them track if their investments are making the intended impact and delivering a solid return on investment. The same principle applies to charitable giving. You should be as good at charitable giving as you are at business. So many people donate their money to charities and have no scope for where their money is going or what level of impact they have. A Factory for Good disrupts this commonality by replacing it with clear, measurable outcomes for each input. It also gives you a positive feedback loop that can, in turn, motivate you to input more for a more significant impact. By demanding clear metrics, you, in turn, get feedback on your inputs and can ensure that an organization is measuring itself against its mission.

Some people I interviewed demonstrated extreme discipline in giving once they decided to give. They recognized that writing blank checks to good causes is one approach to a legacy, but it likely will be short-lived. By avoiding giving sporadically or randomly, you will be able to focus your resources on a cause that is sustaining and has a lasting impact. Once you give, hold yourself and the organization you donate to accountable by measuring the impact of your donation. Tracking the effect by recording the number of individuals assisted via what means can help you be further disciplined in future giving efforts, always making sure you have the impact you originally intended.

## When Measuring Impact Becomes a North Star

Cotopaxi, a successful outdoor apparel company, is an excellent example of how to measure the impact of their Factory for Good. Founded in 2013, Cotopaxi was designed as a vehicle to fight extreme poverty through the sale of sustainably designed outdoor products. Specifically, they focus on values-driven governance, creating and protecting value across their value chain, diversity and inclusion, environmental impacts, carbon neutrality, and effective corporate philanthropy. Focused on a clear mission, everyone involved knows what they stand for and what they want future generations to understand about what they cared about. Without a purpose, they would fail in so many areas, but their clear mission—to fight extreme poverty—acts as the North Star for why they exist and translates to great success.

Cotopaxi has given over three million dollars to vetted organizations, and each year, they dedicate at least one percent of revenues to nonprofits that help communities in poverty. This alone is measurable in the amount they choose to give. However, they continue their measurements there.

Each year, they compile an "Impact Report" to track and report on donations and, more importantly, their impacts on those communities.

They do this by tracking each donation by organization, location, area of focus, and amount given. They then enumerate the number of people assisted either directly or indirectly and the form of assistance their donation took. By the end of the year, they can see the total giving amount, the percentage of company revenue given, and the total amount of people assisted.

One employee closely monitored the yearly impact report and deeply understood Cotopaxi's values. When a batch of water-damaged jackets couldn't be sold, she was told that to issue an insurance claim, she had to show proof of destruction, meaning she would have to destroy the jackets personally. Because she was aligned with Cotopaxi's mission, she knew that this wouldn't align with their sustainability values. Instead, she worked with the insurance companies to accept proof of donation instead of destruction, and she was able to donate all of the jackets to local refugee camps. They tracked these donations on their yearly impact report. Furthermore, they established an insurance pathway to donations over destruction for them and other companies.

Cotopaxi can tailor their giving year to year by having a clear, measurable impact. They also have a shared resource to which all employees can point and take pride. This further motivates giving and increases their impact via their Factory for Good.

Another way that Cotopaxi ensures lasting impact is by building long-term relationships with the charities they donate to, as opposed to simply writing blank checks. Over time, they can see those organizations' quality and sophistication go up, and they can see a qualitative impact in addition to their quantitative ones.

*Figure 18-2 Portion of 2023 Cotopaxi Impact Report*

| Org | Grant Activity Location | Area of Focus | Amount Given | Number of People Assisted | Form of Assistance |
|---|---|---|---|---|---|
| J-PAL | Central America | Livelihoods | $75,000 | 2022: 292 | Gender equity research |
| Mercy Corps | Venezuela | Health | $70,000 | 5,148 total | Medical supplies, etc. |
| Mona Foundation | Brazil, Panama, Guatemala | Education | $60,000 | 7,600 total (2,278 direct, 5,322 indirect) | Direct school support |
| Range of Motion Project | Ecuador, Guatemala | Health | $80,000 | 561 direct | Prosthetic care and community rehabilitation |

*Figure 18-3 Totals Section of 2023 Cotopaxi Impact Report*

| | |
|---|---|
| Total FY23 Giving Amount (Global Uprising dba Cotopaxi to The Cotopaxi Foundation)* | $1,275,390 |
| Total FY23 percentage of product revenue given** | 1% |
| Total FY23 Grantmaking Amount (The Cotopaxi Foundation to grantee partners) | $1,481,900 |
| Total FY23 percentage of company revenue granted out to organizations | 1.06% |
| Total FY23 contributions remaining in the Cotopaxi Foundation grant fund as cash to be deployed | $0 |
| Total Number of People Assisted through foundation grants (Directly & Indirectly)*** | 477,090 |
| Total FY23 grantmaking dollars created through Cotopaxi Customer donations | $87,945 |

## Simple Metrics Go a Long Way

Likewise, Bloom, a social-impact insourcing staffing company, measures the impact of their efforts through an annual impact report. Bloom founders see themselves as equal members of the planet and strongly desire to level the playing field to give the impoverished an equal chance at opportunity. They created a company to do just that, building a mission to impact people. Their model for measuring this impact is even simpler. They have just two key metrics that keep them accountable: jobs created and average income growth for employees compared to their previous jobs. These are the metrics that act as their company's North Star throughout the year and when determining how much impact they are realizing in the areas in which they are deployed. In 2023, they created over 1,400 jobs in sixty-seven countries and saw a 2.6x average income growth. That's no small thing! And they're just getting started.

To further enrich the numbers and give perspective to their actual impact, Bloom also reports on qualitative data, including testimonials from those who have received a job through Bloom. Roselle Molina, a team member from the Philippines, shares:

> *Before joining Bloom, my life revolved around a draining routine, which included enduring two to three hours of mind-numbing traffic every day. By the time I got home, I was exhausted. Working for Bloom helped me experience a truly transformative turn. Suddenly, I had more time for myself and my loved ones, and the commute was replaced by the comfort of working from home. The increased income alleviated financial stress and empowered me to pursue one of my biggest dreams—building a home for my family. Now, I enjoy a better work-life*

*balance. Bloom has catalyzed positive change, allowing me to*
*achieve my goals.*

Measuring your impact doesn't require a large-scale operation. Whether you're a successful company or an individual with a passion for a cause, you have the power to measure and amplify your impact. No matter the size of your contribution, it's essential to understand the ripple effect of your actions. You can be your own Factory for Good.

## The Davidson Family

Each year, the Davidson Family creates an annual family giving report. They measure their impact through the amount given, the number of organizations supported, and the breakdown of their contributions across their core values of the environment, education, and humanitarian work. In 2023, they specifically tracked their impact across their three goals of picking up trash in the environment, educating people, and providing food and water.

*Figure 18-4 The Davidson Family Impact Report*

| Grant/Program | Amount given | Impact | Form of assistance |
|---|---|---|---|
| Coding for girls | $5,000 | Sponsored 20 girls to attend an all week coding camp to empower girls to enter the STEM world | Education |
| 5k for food | $1,000 | Our whole family signed up for a 5k where all proceeds go to help feeding the hungry. 75 families were fed. | Food and water |
| Tony Finau's scholarship | $7,500 | Through Tony's foundation we supported 200 students get school supplies and further their education | Education |
| UNICEF | $2,500 | Through Unicef's programs we were able to feed 10 families for the year. | Food and water |
| Grove | $5,000 | They cleared and cleaned an area to plant 2,000 mangrove trees in Florida. Equating to over 1,000 pounds of plastic removed from the wild. | Cleaning up our environment |
| Project Highway | $1,000 | A team of people spent 4 months every saturday picking up trash on the side of the road. Picking up over 10,000 pounds of trash. | Cleaning up our environment |

| $180,606 | 18,178 | 39,000 LBS |
|---|---|---|
| Total Giving | Total Number of people impacted | Pounds of trash picked up |

As you find a cause that is personal to you, gain your own experience, and have discipline, you will be able to create a vehicle for sustaining impact— Good. While this is an accomplishment, it becomes even more potent as you involve your family in how to build a Factory for Good.

# | 19 |

# Extend Your Impact

The impact a Factory for Good has on your legacy is twofold: the actual change your factory makes to the cause to which you are contributing and the involvement of your family in your values and actions, which can leave a lasting impression on them and future generations.

Here's an example of how the Rojas family used their Factory for Good to "help our kids focus on others and be service-oriented." When each child turns twelve, they give them $1,000 to engage with a charity they feel passionate about. Each child is then asked to do a thorough research project exploring the causes they'd like to get involved with, present to the family why they want to support a specific cause and dedicate some time and money to the cause they have decided to support.

The father of the Rojas family told us in his own words how it is going:

> It was a huge success. Our kids loved it! We started with our
> oldest, and when his younger siblings saw what he was doing,

*their twelfth birthday became a big deal and something every-
one was looking forward to.*

*We decided to increase the grant to $5,000 when they turn
sixteen and $10,000 when they turn eighteen. What started as
a way to help our kids focus on giving of themselves and not
concentrate on themselves turned into a multi-year giving boot
camp. Now that most of our kids are older, they've naturally
become active in our family giving strategy. We constantly
talk about ways we want to give our time and money away
effectively.*

*My wife and I love what this has evolved into: the tradition
of giving established in our family and our relationship with
our kids.*

By meaningfully involving their children in their Factory for
Good from a young age, the Rojas family was able to serve others
at a greater scale and plant seeds of service and altruistic motives in
their family members, which will, in turn, affect their family tree
for generations.

This is the exact opposite of the ticking time bomb mentioned
in an earlier chapter. The ticking time bomb of giving assets
away without any framework negatively affects your family tree.
Whereas involving your family members in a worthwhile cause,
like the Rojas family did, can save your family tree for generations
to come.

Many people I interviewed shared similar experiences involving
their children in service or making it a core pillar of their lives.
One family did one ambitious service project every year. One year,
they went to South Asia to work in a hospital, cleaning, painting,

scrubbing floors, and caring for patients' family members. This experience motivated one of the children to become a doctor herself. Not only did this experience provide an opportunity for the family to come together and serve (which is one of the top things I see people do to improve their relationships), but the children of this family are grown up now, and each one is contributing selflessly to their families and communities.

However, direct involvement in your Factory for Good isn't the only way to pass on your values to your kids and future generations. Shared experiences with your kids as you live your values by direct example is a great way to establish who you are as a family and create meaningful memories with your kids. Many people I interviewed pointed to this as the main perk of having time and money. Spending quality time with their families, through a variety of different outlets was priceless.

Connor shares, "The best thing we did was to buy a house in St. George." In this idyllic resort community in southern Utah, he uses the house for family get-togethers, hiking trips, and boating excursions. He has eighteen grandkids, and it's been amazing to have family time and family experiences. He shares, "I thought a second home was a waste of money, but the dedicated time together as a family makes it special."

Another family places value on quality time outdoors. They have a special camping spot near a mountain river where they spend each summer holiday barbecuing and tubing down the river. While the output is enjoyable for all participants, it also has a way of conveying core values like protecting and taking care of the environment and being kind and welcoming to all. This river spot has become a coveted space for the family in a tradition that has endured for generations.

One family in our area values literature and the arts, so they participate every year in the Utah Shakespeare Festival in Cedar City,

Utah. For many summers, they've come together to swim, picnic, and attend the plays and activities around the festival. Through this experience, the values of literature and the arts are emphasized, and the family can create core memories and traditions that may be passed on for years to come.

An innovative way to pass on your values in addition to your assets is an ethical will, also known as a legacy letter. In it, you share your most important values, beliefs, life lessons, and personal wishes with your loved ones. It's a chance to impart non-material inheritances, such as wisdom and moral guidance. It can contain a set of principles you want your heirs to live by as you leave your Factory for Good to them to own and operate.

Finally, the greatest legacy you might leave is your own life story. It can be passed along by your descendants and live on forever. My great-grandfather, Monte L. Bean, left behind what is to us a priceless autobiography. Several useful services exist now that make it so much easier to record stories than it used to be. With a simple app that prompts you daily, you can create a family story that can easily be shared with those you love. It's a book my family and I treasure and refer to often because it teaches so many powerful life lessons and explains in detail how he dealt with massive challenges in successfully building a business and a family. Instead of seeing my great-grandpa as where he landed, he was able to teach us about how hard he had worked to get there. We learned that it took work and that we would also have to work hard to get ahead. Anything he left behind, we weren't entitled to. Even though his money isn't in the family anymore, we understood we didn't earn it. He, however, had worked eighteen-hour days for it.

The first line of the book reads, "Something was wrong!" He then tells a harrowing story from his childhood about a cougar that woke him up while he was camping in the mountains with his family. This story foreshadows the many stirring trials he faced and overcame in his life, like losing a fortune in the stock market crash of 1929 and helping his son through a vicious attack of polio. He dedicated the book,

> "With great love to my children, my grandchildren, and to generations of children I will never know . . . perhaps they will learn something of their family history, become aware of their present heritage, and catch a glimmer of their several possible futures."

Many of my great-grandfather's assets have been dissipated over the years, but his life story remains perhaps the most precious asset he could have left us. It is an incomparable legacy of love.

These are all incredible ways to involve your family in your Factory for Good and ensure your values and impact for good lives beyond you when you pass. Your legacy is the long shadow cast by your lived values and the contributions you make to the world. It is shaped today with every act of kindness, every commitment to justice, and every effort to educate and uplift. Through consciously planning and cultivating your legacy, you ensure that your life's work continues to inspire and make a difference long into the future.

By avoiding the time bomb of shared assets, intently focusing on building a Factory for Good that matters to you, measuring the impact of that factory, and engaging your family in your efforts, you will meet the last crucial step in retooling your factory into one that produces Good, and ultimately extend your impact.

# | 20 |

# Conclusion: What Will Your Factory Be?

Navigating the emotional side of money is both real and exciting. As I've interviewed others and learned from their experiences, I've discovered that I am not alone in my feelings regarding the climb of Money Mountain and transitioning off. These issues are real and tangible to many, and learning how to navigate the emotional complexities of money is crucial to finding fulfillment and lasting happiness.

But I also learned that you do not need to have excess money for the principles of a Factory for Good to apply to you. We all can leverage the frameworks of purpose, relationships, and legacy to take our time, energy, and value and make an enduring Factory for Good.

At only six years old, when a young girl heard her dad was trying to raise some money to assist a family friend who was recently diagnosed with cancer, she was heartbroken. She went to her piggy bank and pulled out everything she had. She humbly asked her dad, "Will this be enough to help your friend?" The total was $5.12. This simple act of kindness brought her dad to tears. He took the money and added it to the fund for his friend, but the ripple effect of that moment was extensive. Out of all the donations to the cancer fund, that small act of $5.12, in many ways, held the most value. It represented everything that a young person had.

This young girl's dad, Nick, created a charity named the Five.12 Foundation in the spirit of her donation. He has rallied volunteers to package meals for schoolchildren to take home on weekends. Many elementary school students in the United States go home from school on Friday and return hungry on Monday. Five.12 provides weekend backpacks full of food for those students in need. Five.12 is one hundred percent volunteer run, and one hundred percent of donations (both time and money) provide food for needy students. But it's mostly funded by Nick himself. He realizes that the more money he makes in his factory, the more good he can do. He has found a deep passion in taking his profits from business and in turn leveraging them to do Good.

A small act of kindness had a ripple effect and turned into a full-fledged Factory for Good.

You don't need to start a charity or engage with a nonprofit to create a Factory for Good. You can get started in your own home and community. In one case, Lorene lived a more modest lifestyle throughout her career to have more resources for doing good in the world. Even when she could afford to do so financially, she refrained from buying a new car or designer clothes. Instead, Lorene saved everything after she paid for bills and essentials and put it into a fund to help those she saw in need around her. She took it upon herself to be the neighborhood caretaker. She tried to learn everybody's names and circumstances to be an agent of service and good in her community. She would always be on the lookout for someone who needed a warm meal, a single mom who needed a car payment, or a cause that needed donations. While she sometimes included monetary funds, she mostly donated her time and energy, and her impact was felt throughout the community.

For those with excess, money acts only as an amplifier to the good you can do. It's crucial to know when to move from money as your output to something that positively impacts your family and the world.

And that's why I wrote this book—as a call to action—as much for myself as for others.

I can either find a higher purpose and fulfill it, or not.

I can cultivate deep relationships that matter, or not.

I can establish a lasting legacy for my posterity and in my community, or not.

And so can you. Like my grandfather and great-grandfather, myself, and anyone in this life, the choice is yours.

My grandfather didn't set out to destroy his legacy, relationships, purpose, and, ultimately, wealth. But he did. In deciding to do nothing but continue in his money-making business, he was left blindsided and alone, a fate I would wish upon no one.

Likewise, my great-grandfather didn't necessarily set out to cultivate his purpose, relationships, and legacy. But by intentionally changing his output at the end of his factory line to create opportunity for his family and those around him, by looking outward instead of inward, my great-grandfather was able to masterfully establish a Factory for Good that still exists to this day. Just last year, I had a man whom I had never met reach out to me to tell me what an incredible impact my great-grandfather had on his life. Almost fifty years later, his impact is still deeply felt. I was humbled by his description of my great-grandfather and the resonating effect that he still had on this man and his family's life.

And that's the real power in the Factory for Good. When done right (and I desperately hope that I outlined ways to do it right), it won't just fundamentally change your own life. It will change many lives—the lives of your loved ones, and their loved ones, and their loved ones. A ripple effect that has the potential to endure for countless generations.

This—the act of a single individual impacting those around them and their family tree—is the world's most potent perpetrator of good. It can do more good than any large organization burdened by politics and bureaucracy. Each individual can be the critical difference in lasting change to natural causes worldwide.

Think of the most impactful person you know. Now, imagine you multiplied that person's resources tenfold. Imagine the impact that they could have. Now imagine ten of that person, one hundred, 1,000!

This is the power of establishing an enduring Factory for Good by retooling your current life factory. Navigating through these stages involves more than just managing your emotional response. It requires you to engage actively with the world in new ways, leveraging your skills, passions, and resources to fulfill your own needs and contribute positively to the lives of others. This is the essence of building a Factory for Good—transforming your capabilities into actions that generate lasting, meaningful impacts.

As you transition your factory's focus from producing money to creating Good, remember that this journey is highly individual. What works for one person may not work for another. The key is to stay true to your values, remain flexible in your methods, and be patient with yourself as you explore new terrains of purpose and engagement.

Retooling your factory isn't just about changing what you produce but redefining how you see yourself and your role in the world. It's about moving from success to significance, from achieving personal goals to empowering others, earning a living, and making a life that resonates with the deepest parts of who you are.

This journey, though filled with challenges, is enriching. By embracing the changes and opportunities that come with each stage, you position yourself to thrive and leave a legacy of good that extends far beyond your own life. It's about making a difference, one action at a time, and seeing your factory as a source of personal fulfillment and broad-scale impact.

I want to protect my family tree, resemble the life of my great-grandpa, and have a Factory for Good that endures beyond my existence and primary circle of influence. In doing so, I will generate a positive, lasting impact.

I'll be happy if I can help even one other person use these frameworks to amplify how they manage their time, energy, and money in the sincere pursuit of output for good. I've seen what happens to one person who doesn't, and I want to help others avoid the pitfalls that lead to that ending, if possible.

I've researched, shared the stories of those doing it, and combined what matters into actionable frameworks. The pillars of purpose, relationships, and legacy are yours to read, study, apply, and share.

Whether you are at the peak of your success or just starting your journey, now is the time to build your own Factory for Good.

# APPENDIX

# What Should You Do Next?

Thank you for taking the time to read this book. It has been a passion of mine, and I am hopeful that by sharing my work with you, we will be able to increase the number of Factories for Good in the world. If you enjoyed *Factory for Good: the Pitfalls of Prosperity and How to Avoid Them* you might be interested in other content geared toward navigating the emotional complexities of money. The latest content is available on a free platform called the *Factory*.

Subscribers are the first to hear about new content and projects and are included in an exclusive network of other high-net-worth individuals.

While there are many exercises available on the online platform, we've included the ones mentioned as part of the book in this Appendix. Feel free to access expanded versions of these exercises online as well.

You can sign up here:
http://www.factoryforgood.com/

# The Happiness Audit

The "Happiness Audit" is a powerful tool designed to help you pinpoint and embrace the sources of authentic joy in your life. Sometimes, our assumptions about what brings us happiness are only surface-level; this exercise encourages you to go deeper, identify the source of your joy, and quantify how much it actually affects your life for the better.

Dedicate some quiet time to ponder the following:

**List what gives you happiness.** Consider various aspects of your life (e.g., work, home relationships, hobbies, etc.) and type out everything that brings you happiness on a spreadsheet. These brainstorming questions may help you:

- Who in your life never fails to lift your spirits? What do you do together that makes you happy?
- Are there specific locations, whether a room in your house, a nearby park, or a far-off country, where you feel happiest?
- What holidays, traditions, or celebrations resonate with you the most?
- Are there particular sounds, tastes, sights, smells, or feelings that elevate your mood? What activities and habits reliably make you happy?

- What are some daily habits, experiences, or indulgences that make your day?
- What are some accomplishments or milestones, big or small, that have given you a sense of pride or joy?

**Categorize these things** as an experience, possession, relationship, or other.

**Assign to each item a value from one to seven**, reflecting the level of joy it brings you. One is not much happiness at all, while seven is complete contentment.

**Consider duration.** How long does each source of happiness last? Are we talking about a quick shot of dopamine (short), a sustained feeling of contentment (medium), or a profound and lasting fulfillment (long)?

**Assign a cost** from one dollar sign to four dollar signs to each item. Zero is free and four is very expensive.

**Ponder your answers.** Now that you have all this information, what does it tell you about what makes you happy? Consider:

- What are the top three sources of joy in your life?
- What is the average cost of the things that bring you the most happiness?
- How much joy do the most expensive things bring you?
- What is something that surprised you?

This process serves as a powerful reminder of what truly brings you happiness. This exercise is actually helpful at whatever stage of life you are in. Taking the Happiness Audit every so often is a great way to check in with yourself and evaluate if you're living life in a way that will make you truly happy. The results may or may not surprise you. Either way, this exercise can guide you toward the aspects of your life you should focus on the most.

# The Bank of Mom and Dad

The "Bank of Mom and Dad" is a great way to put into writing your family bank's agreements in the form of a bank charter. The charter defines how the bank will serve the family's needs. It lays out how the family will make decisions, solve problems, resolve conflicts, and govern the institution. It rests on the family's values and goals, how they will handle financial transactions, philanthropy, and so forth. The charter should:

- Describe a vision for the bank, its objectives, and its values.
- Define a code of conduct for family members concerning the bank.
- Create a group that directs bank activity and outlines expectations for this group.
- Define, in general, how transactions will be handled, such as deposits, loans, taxes, and dividends. This definition might include the bank's philosophy on payment schedules, interest rates, defaults, and so forth.
- Include rules based on the child's age to determine what you as parents are responsible for and what the child is responsible for; in other words, who's going to pay for what and when?

You and your partner should work together to create the bank charter. Once you have alignment, you can share it with the kids. There are two big advantages here: First, the kids know what to expect, and second, you and your partner can use the family bank discussion to get on the same page about how to finance your family. Basic principles of banking, like balancing income and outgo and managing cash flow, don't have to be burdensome. Because children need to understand those principles anyway, use the "Bank of Mom and Dad" as a teaching tool. To help you get started, here is a sample template for a family bank charter:

# The {Insert Family Name] Bank Charter

This bank's goal is to provide the {insert family name} family access to opportunity, have unique experiences, and grow closer as a family. Anything contrary to this will not be supported by the Bank of Mom and Dad(BoMD). You can access this because Mom and Dad love and want to help you live a full life.

**What the Bank of Mom and Dad will Pay for:**
{Outline something you are willing to pay for i.e. $75 a month for gas money}

**How to request capital?**
{What is the process you want your kids to ask for money? Is it all the same process or do bigger requests require a written proposal?}

**Incentives**
{What are ways you are rewarding good habits? i.e. Investment match}

**Overspending:**
{What happens when there is overspending? Outline the consequences.}

**Gift Money (e.g. birthdays, holidays):**
{Outline exceptions to the rule with gifts}

**Record Keeping:**
{How do you expect the exchange of funds to be tracked?}

**Loans and Grants:**
{If your child needs money for a car, school, a down payment outlining whether or not you expect interest to be paid.}

**Financial Education:**
{Is there any training or specific conversations you want to have with your kid? Have a specific outline.}

**Revision of Rules:**
{How often do you want to revisit the terms of this agreement? Annually is usually enough. It is a great time to remind of expectations.}

# The Loan Agreement

The "Loan Agreement" is a great resource to have on hand when family members come asking for money. If you choose to lend any amount (as opposed to freely gifting the money), then having a written agreement will help hold you both accountable to the loan terms. Like a typical bank loan, the Loan Agreement describes the amount, terms, and interest rate as well as a penalty for a late notice. While this agreement could take many different forms, we've provided an example loan agreement for you to replicate here:

# {Insert Family Name} Bank - Loan Agreement

This loan agreement ("Agreement") is made and entered into this ____ day of
_____, 20 ____, by and between  {Insert Family Name} Bank ("Lender") and
_____ ("Borrower").

1. Principal Amount: The Lender agrees to loan the Borrower the sum of
   _____ Dollars ($_____ ).

2. Repayment Term: The Borrower agrees to repay the loaned amount in full
   by the ____ day of _____, 20___.

3. Interest Rate: An interest rate of % per month will be applied to the principal
   amount. Therefore, the Borrower will repay a total amount of $_____
   (principal + interest) by the end of the repayment term.

4. Penalty for Late Payment: If the Borrower fails to repay the loan by the
   agreed-upon date, an additional penalty of _____ Dollars
   ($_____) will be applied for each month the loan remains unpaid.

5. Miscellaneous:
   • The Borrower acknowledges that they have read, understood, and agree
     to the terms set forth in this Agreement.
   • This Agreement is intended to promote trust and understanding and is
     not legally binding in a court of law, but is binding in the Court of Mom
     and Dad. If the terms here are not met (paid back), then the Bank of
     Mom and Dad will not loan or help financially again.

**Borrower**                    **Mom**                    **Dad**

Name: _____      Name: _____      Name: _____

Date: _____      Date: _____      Date: _____

Signature:    .              Signature:                Signature:

_____          _____          _____

# The Factory for Good Finder

The "Factory for Good Finder" is a great exercise to help you determine where, how, and why you want to make an impact. Use the values wheel to complete the following exercise.

**Determine *Where* You Want to Make an Impact**

1. Choose three triangles from the center circle that you care about the most.
2. For each of your top three sections, choose two branches of the middle circle.
3. Choose two branches in the outer circle for each of your top three sections.

If it's hard to start with your three core values, feel free to reverse the order and start with the outer circle and work your way in. The circle is designed to meet you where you're at.

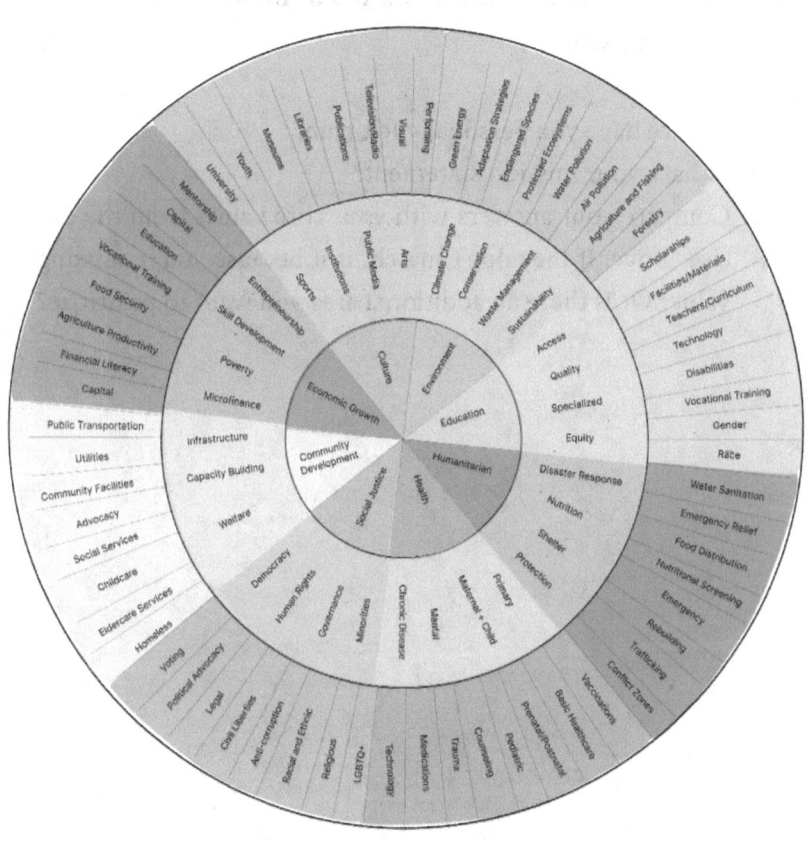

**Determine *How* You Want to Make an Impact**

Answer for yourself:

1. What experiences with worthwhile causes have you had that you liked? What did you like about them? Any that you don't like?
2. What outcomes/measurements are you looking to achieve?

**Determine *Why* You Want to Make an Impact**

Answer for yourself:

1. Where have you personally felt pain?
2. What's your mission statement?
3. Compare your answers with your core values from the exercise above. If they don't match, is it because you're missing a value? Or is there an additional area you want to prioritize?

# The Impact Score

The "Impact Score" is a way to determine what impact a donation (of time or money) will have and is a tool to compare one donation to another before committing any amount. While you may find it useful to come up with your own score, here is what we use in our Factory for Good.

There is a potential of 15 points to be earned for each potential donation. Go through and tally your points according to the description below to arrive at your respective impact score. For each donation, you will land anywhere from 0–15 points, with 15 being the highest impact.

- 1 pt - for each value it hits (3 potential)

- Points for the level of people assisted (5 potential)
    - 1 pt very low: 1 person

    - 2 pts low: 2–10 people

    - 3 pts medium: 10–25 people

    - 4 pts large: 25–100 people

    - 5 pts very large: 100+

- Points for fundamentally changing each person's life (5 potential)
  - 5 pts very high

  - 4 pts high

  - 3 pts medium

  - 2 pts low

  - 1 pt very low

- 1 pt if it involves the family

- 1 pt my gut tells me it's impactful/personal to me

Add up all the points, then place it aside your donation in your records. If you decide to donate, make sure to include the impact score on your impact report so you can hold yourself accountable to the anticipated level of impact.

# The Impact Report

The "Impact Report" is how you can measure the impact of your factory. I interviewed Cotopaxi's leaders to find out how you could create your own "FFG Impact Report," a representation of how your Factory for Good is influencing the world around you. Whether you're giving a lot or a little, the report can help you engage and excite you and your family about doing good.

In this Impact Report, you focus on the impact created rather than the money returned. What are the goals of your Factory for Good? What key numbers will show whether those goals are being met? Here are a few guidelines for creating a Family Impact Report:

**Select carefully the organizations to which you want to contribute.** Make sure they are aligned with your values and you are comfortable with their accountability systems as we've reviewed above. The size of the organization and the check will determine how much leverage you have, but make your expectations clear from the start.

**List your impact goals in terms of people helped or needs served.** As you measure the size of your impact, it's important to be conscious of guiding your goals to the outcomes you want to see. Impact, in this case, isn't measured in return on your investment in terms of quantifiable funds. Make sure they quantify the size of the impact coupled with a timing of when this impact should occur.

**Track progress regularly and often.** Create a scoreboard so you can see progress. It's easy to lose sight of your goals unless you check in periodically to see how things are going. For example, if you're funding an agency to create internships, ask them to brief you regularly on the numbers. If they fall behind on your goal, ask them what you can do to help remove obstacles to progress. It also helps to assign an impact score (from 1 to 15) based on the perceived impact each donation will have. This way, you can compare impact scores for each contribution.

**Reflect on your results annually.** An annual "board meeting" is a great time to look back at the impact report and reflect on what your Factory for Good has been able to accomplish and what you want to accomplish next year. This allows your factory to be enduring and sustaining, always improving and growing according to your values and goals. Below is an example report from a Factory for Good that you can use as a template in crafting your Factory for Good Impact Report.

| Organization | Area of Focus | Amount Given | Number of People Assisted | Form of Assistance | Impact Score |
|---|---|---|---|---|---|
| Local University | Education | $100,000 | 5 | Paid Internships | 7 |
| Service Abroad | Education | $50,000 | 10 | Paid Internships | 8 |
| Rescue Committee | Humanitarian | $25,000 | 25 | Shelter | 6 |
| **TOTALS:** | | $175,000 | 35 | **AVERAGE:** | 7 |

# The Factory for Good Template

The "Factory for Good Template" is a framework to run through different causes as you come across them. It will help you determine who they are, who you'll help, how it aligns with your core values, and the different impact options you have. If you can't successfully fill this template out, you probably shouldn't be donating to a particular cause. Here is a fictitious example of our template filled out to help you get started:

**Factory: Feast of Hope**

https://websitelink.com

- Is Performance Measured? YES
- Is It Legitimate? YES
- Is it Value Aligned? YES

WHO WE ARE

Feast of Hope is a foundation dedicated to the eradication of hunger in the United States.

Feast of Hope Foundation is a visionary organization dedicated to eradicating hunger and fostering nutritional well-being across the nation. With a belief that access to nutritious food is a fundamental human right, Feast of Hope operates on the principles of compassion, innovation, and community collaboration. Our initiatives span from local food drives and sustainable agricultural projects to national partnerships aimed at enhancing food security and dietary health. By mobilizing a network of volunteers, donors, and experts, we strive to create a world where no individual faces the uncertainty of their next meal.

WHO YOU'LL HELP

83% more meals donated at a national level
77% less children going hungry each year

WHERE YOU'LL HELP
National

HOW WE'RE DIFFERENT
Our approach is holistic, addressing not only the immediate needs for food but also the underlying causes of hunger, such as poverty, inequality, and climate change. Feast of Hope Foundation envisions a future where communities thrive with access to ample, nutritious food, ensuring that every table has a feast of hope.

# IMPACT OPTIONS

| Amount | Donation Type | Impact Score |
|--------|---------------|--------------|
| $10 | Donate a Meal | 4 |
| $750 | Feed a family for a week | 6 |
| $1K | Foster a rural farmer (connect to markets) | 8 |
| $10K | Fund a food waste initiative in 1 city | 6 |
| $100K | Donate needed farm equipment | 9 |
| $300K | Complete a solar panel project | 7 |

# The Legacy Letter

The "Legacy Letter" is a great exercise to complete to pass down your core values and wishes to your posterity.

A great way to start a legacy letter is to try an experiment. Think of 3–7 adjectives that you think people would use to describe you, ways that you would be remembered after you pass. Then write down 3–7 adjectives that you *wish* they would say. For example, I completed this exercise and came up with the following:

| Actual List | Wish List |
| --- | --- |
| Selfish | Lived a life of service |
| Competitive | He was an influence for good |
| Had good friends | Loved unconditionally |

Compare the two. If there are differences, take some time to reflect on why. What characteristics and values do you want to live by so they are what people remember about your life? These characteristics can guide how you live your life but can also serve as the foundation when considering writing a legacy letter for your posterity. These are the same characteristics and values that will carry weight when you pass.

As you share your most important values, beliefs, life lessons, and personal wishes with your loved ones, either through a letter or by example, you are more likely to ensure that they live through a lasting legacy.

# REFERENCES

## Prologue

Baumeister, R. F., & Vohs, K. D. (2020). Does helping promote a sense of meaning? The Journal of Positive Psychology.

Tsipursky, G. (2020). Is serving others the key to meaning and purpose? Psychology Today.

Pogosyan, M. (2017). In helping others, you help yourself. Psychology Today.

Editorial Staff. (2015). 7 scientific benefits of helping others. Mental Floss.

## Chapter 1: The Factory

Maslow, A. H. (1943). A theory of human motivation. Psychological Review, 50(4), 370-396.

Williams, L., & Lumen Learning. (n.d.). Factors of production: Inputs and outputs. In Introduction to Business. Tidewater Community College.

## Chapter 2: Earning Your Sleep

Aristotle. (350 B.C.E). Metaphysics. In W. D. Ross (Trans.).

Rotary International. (n.d.). Ending Polio

We Are For Good. (2023). Below the Surface of charity: water's $700M Impact - Scott Harrison. We Are For Good.


## Chapter 3: The Path to the Peak

WorldAtlas. (2021). Mount Rainier.

Bisceglio, P. (2013). Sixty Years Ago, Edmund Hillary Reached the Top of the World. Smithsonian Magazine.

Silvestre, D. (n.d.). Managing Oneself by Peter Drucker: Summary and Notes.


## Chapter 4: The Disease of More

Riley, P. (1994). The Winner Within: A Life Plan for Team Players. New York, NY: Putnam Publishing Group.

WHUR. (2021, November 10). Oprah And Will Smith Talk All About How He Almost Lost It All.

Seneca. (n.d.). Moral Letters to Lucilius (Letter 17).

Psychology Today. (n.d.). Hedonic Treadmill.

Thiel, P., & Masters, B. (2014). Zero to One: Notes on Startups, or How to Build the Future. Crown Business.

## Chapter 6: The 4 Stages of What's Next

Moynes, R. (2022). The Four Phases of Retirement: What to Expect When You're Retiring. Ontario: Moynes Publishing.

Reiner, R. (Director). (2007). The Bucket List [Film]. Warner Bros.

Brooks, A. C. (2022). From Strength to Strength: Finding Success, Happiness, and Deep Purpose in the Second Half of Life. Portfolio.

Grant, U. S. (1885). Personal Memoirs of U.S. Grant. New York: Charles L. Webster & Company.

Heaton, P. (2020). Your Second Act: Inspiring Stories of Reinvention. Simon & Schuster.

Edison, T. A. (1910). Edison: His Life and Inventions. New York: Harper & Brothers.

Crow, B. (2021). You Just Have to Grab the Next Trapeze: A Former Lawyer Reinvents Himself After Escaping to France. In C. Guillebeau, Optimal Work Daily [Podcast].

## Chapter 7: The Happiness Audit

Frankl, V. E. (1946). Man's Search for Meaning. Beacon Press.

## Chapter 8: Living Life In Crescendo

Covey, S. R., & Covey Haller, C. (2022). Live Life in Crescendo: Your Most Important Work Is Always Ahead of You. Simon & Schuster.

Rosen, H. (2024). The Transformation of Tangelo Park. In It's My View.

Steinberg, M. (2024). Steinberg on Beethoven's Symphony No. 9.

## Chapter 9: The Only Thing That Really Matters

O'Neal, S. (2024). "I'm in a 100,000 square-foot house by myself." The Big Podcast with Shaq.

Lifespan Research Foundation. (2024). History of the Harvard Study of Adult Development.

Psychology Today. (2024). Do Half of All Marriages Really End in Divorce?

American Academy of Matrimonial Lawyers. (n.d.).

Levine, M. (2006). The Price of Privilege: How Parental Pressure and Material Advantage Are Creating a Generation of Disconnected and Unhappy Kids. HarperCollins.

Christensen, C. M. (2010). How Will You Measure Your Life?. Harvard Business Review.

Financial Freedom Countdown. (2024). What Is Generational Wealth And How To Build And Pass It Down.

## Chapter 10: Protecting Your Marriage in Prosperity

Friedman, R. (2018, March 23). A Doctor's Dying Wish. The New York Times.

## Chapter 11: The Bank of Mom and Dad

EisnerAmper. (2019). Family Business - Creating a Family Charter.

## Chapter 13: Investing in Emotional Capital

Purdue University. (2018, February 13). Money only buys happiness for a certain amount. ScienceDaily.

Biddulph, S. (2018). Raising Boys in the 21st Century: How to Help Our Boys Become Open-Hearted, Kind, and Strong Men.

Thagard, P. (n.d.). Emotional Capital. Psychology Today.

Rampage, C. (2016, August 22). Mental Health of Affluent Teens: The Challenge of Prosperity. Counseling@Northwestern.

Obama, M. (2018). Becoming. Crown Publishing Group.

## Chapter 14: The Speed Bumps of Change

LightBloomers. (2023, August 10). A healthy person has a thousand wishes, a sick person just one.

Reader's Digest. (2019, November 7). Beautiful Proverbs About Life from Around the World. Reader's Digest.

## Chapter 15: The Ticking Time Bomb

Munger, Charlie. Interview by John Cassidy. "Of Course It Will," Charlie Said. "But You Still Have to Do It." The New Yorker, 1 May 2016.

Bill Perkins, Die with Zero: Getting All You Can from Your Money and Your Life. Mariner Books, 2020.

Davis, Chris. Interview by William Green. "Ambassador Shelby C. Davis, a Legendary Investor and Founder of the Philanthropic Davis Funds."

Richer, Wiser, Happier: How the World's Greatest Investors Win in Markets and Life. Scribner, 2021

## Chapter 16: The Ripple Effect

Miranda, Lin-Manuel. Hamilton: An American Musical. 2015.

Kristof, Nicholas D., and Sheryl WuDunn. Tightrope: Americans Reaching for Hope. Knopf, 2020.

Carnegie, Andrew. The Autobiography of Andrew Carnegie and The Gospel of Wealth. Signet Classics, 2006.

## Chapter 17: What Good Looks Like

Norwich, William. The Gilded Age: A Tale of Today. Simon & Schuster, 1997.

## Chapter 18: How to Build a Factory for Good

Personal Conversations with Joseph Grenny, author of Crucial Conversations and a co-builder of the non-profit UNITUS.

Smith, Davis. Do Good: The Cotopaxi Story. HarperOne, 2021.

Personal Conversations with Annie Agle, VP of Impact and Sustainability at Cotopaxi.

Cotopaxi. 2023 Impact Report. Cotopaxi, 2024. Available at: cotopaxi.com/impact.

Bloom. 2023 Impact Report. Hirebloom, 2023. Available at: hire-bloom.com

Personal Conversations with Eric Engebretsen, Co-founder of Bloom.

**Conclusion: What Will Your Factory Be**

Five.12 Foundation. Five.12 Foundation Impact Report 2023. Five.12 Foundation, 2023.

# ACKNOWLEDGEMENTS

This book would not have been possible without the support and contributions of some key individuals.

Megan: you are my Circle A. Everything in my life means more because you're by my side. Thank you for not just always letting me take the risks in life but in believing in me and encouraging me to do so. Much of the content in this book comes from our many conversations on these topics and your overall grounded approach to life and building a true 'Factory for Good.' I love you.

Camden: thank you for the countless hours of brainstorming, planning, writing, editing, executing, discussing, and finalizing everything that went into this book. Many of the ideas within this book were born from conversations with you, or you said directly. Thank you for being there from the beginning.

Hannah: the right person at the right time to come in and get the book to where it is. It's not an understatement to say this book wouldn't have been published if it wasn't for you. Thank you for helping own it and bring it to life.

I would also like to thank my extended family who taught me to be proud of my heritage. To know where I came from and the work that was put into building our family name is something that motivates me almost daily. I'm very proud to come from the family I do. I hope I don't let you down.

Finally, this book is built intentionally and gratefully on the stories of those who have "done it." To all the people I interviewed: thank you for your time, stories, and vulnerability in exposing such personal parts of your life. I really am grateful to call many of you my friends and to have been motivated by your life stories. I hope I captured the essence of what it was you were trying to tell me and I hope you are motivated by the many others that also shared stories, as we all seek to build our own Factory for Good.

www.ingramcontent.com/pod-product-compliance
Lightning Source LLC
Chambersburg PA
CBHW011236120626
46549CB00009B/3284